WESTERN SHERIFFS AND MARSHALS

THOMAS PENFIELD
WESTERN SHERIFFS
AND
MARSHALS

ILLUSTRATED BY ROBERT GLAUBKE

NEW YORK Grosset & Dunlap PUBLISHERS

FOREWORD

THE SCENE IS FAMILIAR—rehearsed countless times in fiction, in the movies, on television and radio, and by elaborately armed small boys from the crowded sidewalks of New York to the backyards of California.

The "good man," his star shining on his chest, faces the "bad man." Both are tall, tanned, broad-shouldered, narrow-hipped, tight-lipped—and afraid of nothing on earth. They exchange a few soft-spoken words in the drawling tones of casual conversation, but the tone can't mask the tension. A lightning sweep of two practiced right arms, the ear-splitting roar of two Colt six-shooters, almost but not quite simultaneous—and the bad man bites the dust of the town's only street.

The story lives on in this rigid form, seldom varied, stripped of all extraneous details of personality and history, for in the endless retelling it has become a full-blown legend, joining the ranks of earlier tales of giants and heroes the world over. To many people abroad, unaware of our other colorful traditions, the legend means America. To Americans in all sections of the country it serves to keep alive the memory of the great adventure that unlocked the vast wealth of the West and extended our traditions of independence from coast to coast.

But a legend can become a bloodless thing as it is stripped of specific times, places, and personalities—a puppet show performed by abstractions such as "the good man" and "the bad man." If the retelling has made the story of frontier justice seem a mere dramatic convention, the truth about the "good men" and the "bad men" of the Old West—none of whom were wholly good or bad—will restore blood to the legend. For the men who made the legend were even more fabulous than their own tall tales and the fiction of the Western movie is a pale reflection of their colorful reality. In this book Tom Penfield has restored to full size a score of the most spectacular of the men whose guns brought law to the West.

Nothing can be added here to the colorful stories the author tells of the men themselves, but their exploits may be more believable when set in the large framework of history.

From the time of the very first settlers, the taming of the frontier was marked by violence. For all its lonely vastness the western part of the continent was by no means an uninhabited country when the first white settlers pushed into it. The many tribes of Indians who roamed over the prairies and mountains needed space—far more space than the white farmer or even the cattle raiser. For the Indians, especially those with whom the settlers had their most savage battles, were hunters. The land cannot produce wild game in the same profusion that it will yield food to the farmer or the herdsman. Thus, while there seemed no end of land to the lonely settlers, the Indians felt crowded quite soon after the white man's rifles began taking their toll of buffalo and deer.

The Indians fought the invaders with more savagery than they had ever shown in their wars with one another. There were massacres and individual atrocities that stun the civilized imagination. But the retaliation by the settlers was not one whit less savage. Replying in kind, they visited their wrath not only upon the warriors but massacred whole villages of Indian women and children, often without seeking to determine if their victims belonged even to the same tribes as the raiders whose attacks they were avenging.

"The only good Indian is a dead Indian" became in many places the only law. It was, in fact, the settlers who introduced the practice of scalping to most of the western tribes. In the earliest days the Spaniards had offered rewards for Apache scalps; the English and French had paid Indians for the scalps of other Indians and many of the colonies in the east had paid bounties to their citizens for Indian scalps. As late as 1814, the Territory of Indiana offered a fifty-dollar reward for every Indian scalp as an "encouragement to the enterprise and bravery of our fellow citizens."

There were always men among both whites and Indians who wanted to stop the slaughter of retaliation, but fear and hatred did not cool easily. In Oregon, for instance, an elderly miner who refused to participate in raids on the Indians' villages was forced to accompany a party of raiding whites, who took him out, shot him, and hung his head in a tree.

Gradually, however, as the settlers became more numerous and more secure, the Indian wars abated, but the appeal to violence was not easily forgotten. The settlers, now numerous enough to tread on each other's toes, hewed to the same law of vengeance and retaliation in settling their own differences. They had deep and bitter differences.

Cattlemen fought sheep ranchers over grass and water, ranchers fought with farmers, big cattle owners fought with smaller ranchers, miners fought over claims, and wild cowboys clashed with the more settled businessmen in the towns that drew their livelihood from the cattle business. Against the background of these conflicts, individual crimes of passion and profit flourished.

The frontier's first form of justice was, quite naturally, personal retaliation. In a region where there was little or no government, where courts were far away, and where land titles and cattle brands were often in dispute, the righting of any man's wrongs was his own responsibility—or if he had died with his boots on, then the duty of retaliation fell to his family and friends. The tragic flaw in such a system of justice is that retaliation invites counter-retaliation, until a whole community becomes swept up into a blood feud. Some of the early feuds wiped out entire families and numbered among their most active partisans the very peace officers whose job it was to prevent such outbreaks.

One of the bitterest of early feuds, which reached almost the point of organized warfare, occurred in Shelby County, Texas, around the middle of the last century. The first blood was let by Charles W. Jackson, a former Mississippi steamboater, a fugitive from justice and an unsuccessful candidate for the Texas Congress. Encountering a political enemy, Joseph G. Goodbread, unarmed, Jackson coolly shot him through the heart after telling his victim of his intention.

Free on bond while waiting for the court to open some months later, Jackson lost no time in gathering about him a following intended to prevent his conviction. He organized a group of armed ruffians under the guise of vigilantes and set out to prevent retaliation among Goodbread's friends by killing them first. Unable to catch Goodbread's friends, he burned their houses. When Jackson's trial came up, his small army managed to scare the judge out of town and win an acquittal for him from the jury without any trial. By this time his group had become known as the Regulators, a term that was applied frequently throughout the West to citizens' groups organized to put down crime.

Meanwhile Goodbread's friends were not idle. They organized a similar group, which became known as the Moderators, whose aim was supposed to be upholding the courts against the tactics of the Regulators. The real aim of the Moderators, however, was to kill Jackson under the code of the feud. For more than three years the warring groups battled each other and terrorized the rest of the citizens of the section. Finally Jackson was ambushed and slain, but such is the nature of a feud that this was not the end. The Regulators retaliated by hanging three of the Moderators, and the war went on until a pitched battle between detachments of the two groups numbering several hundred each was narrowly averted when Marshal Alexander Horton managed to arrange a truce. Even this did not mark the end of the feud, but thereafter it gradually died down. In the four years following the death of Goodbread, about fifty men were killed in the war between the Regulators and the Moderators.

As law enforcement improved such feuds didn't get a chance to blaze up, but the last and the greatest of the Western feuds occurred at the turn of the century after most of the West had become relatively law-abiding. This was the infamous Pleasant Valley war between the Grahams and the Tewksburys in central Arizona's Tonto Basin.

The end of the personal feuds, most of which had died down long before the Pleasant Valley war, did not, however, mean the triumph of law and order. The ranges still knew warfare, but instead of battles of personal retaliation, range warfare became clashes between economic interests. Of these conflicts the greatest was the Johnson County war in 1892. This was no battle of hot-headed Westerners out to avenge the wrong of a friend or brother; it was a planned and calculated invasion of Johnson County, Wyoming, by a small, but lavishly equipped force outfitted by the Wyoming Stock Grower's Association, an organization of the big cattlemen.

The background of the clash followed the pattern of conflict in many parts of the West between the big cattlemen, who grazed their herds far and wide across the public grazing lands, and the small ranchers and farmers who took land under Homestead laws, fenced in the range and, according to the Association, started their own herds with animals rustled from the scattered herds of the big owners.

Following a number of minor skirmishes in which several homesteaders were killed, the big stockmen got the state to agree to seize all cattle on public land bearing the brands of suspected rustlers. The Association's list of such brands included practically all except those belonging to its members. This was the opening gun. In retaliation the small stock growers organized their own association and agreed to hold their roundups ahead of the date set by the state commissioners in order to get their cattle before they were seized.

The cattle barons decided the time had come for a long-talked-of invasion of Johnson County to teach the "rustlers" a lesson.

Secretly, but with the blessing and aid of the acting governor, the cattlemen outfitted a special train and loaded it with a group of cowboys recruited from Texas. It left Cheyenne on April 4, 1892, for Buffalo, the seat of Johnson County to the north. After establishing headquarters at the ranch of one of the Association's members the expedition set out to get two men the Association had clashed with before—Nick Rae and Nathan D. Champion. Rae was cut down as he stepped out the door but Champion was slain only after a day-long siege.

Word of the attack passed quickly and the Johnson Countians under Sheriff W. G. (Red) Angus set out to meet the invasion and finally surrounded the invaders with a superior force on the Harris Ranch. The invaders managed to sneak a man out to telegraph their plight to the governor. And after a three-day siege they were rescued by Federal troops ordered out by President Benjamin Harrison on the governor's plea.

This was perhaps the most spectacular attempt at private "law enforcement" in the West, and for justification its perpetrators drew on a long precedent of law enforcement outside the law. The Johnson County war did not, however, bear any relation to the work of earlier unofficial enforcement groups beyond the fact that neither the Johnson County invaders nor the earlier vigilantes had any authorization in written law.

While the cattlemen's force was bent on enforcing private law for a particular group, the true vigilantes had acted to enforce public law in the community interest. Any kind of law enforcement by private citizens is dangerous and the vigilance committees were undoubtedly guilty of grave injustices, but in the beginning these groups of private citizens took it upon themselves to enforce order because they had no other choice but to submit to chaos.

The vigilance committees were originally the product of the mining camps of California during the Gold Rush. Even had there been adequate forces of able peace officers in the camps, official law enforcement would have been virtually impossible because of the absence of jails. There was simply no safe way to hold a prisoner for trial, so the citizens tried a suspect on the spot and carried out the sentence immediately. In the absence of jails, there were generally only three sentences to choose from—banishment, whipping, or hanging.

Originally the punishment was meted out by the whole community of miners, but as the camps grew larger the responsibility was delegated to a group of the most influential men in the camp. This vigilance committee or miners' court was directly responsive to public opinion. It had to be, for no group of men could be found willing to cross a whole camp of irate miners.

It was in the metropolis of San Francisco where hordes of criminals mingled with honest adventurers—who, themselves, were certainly not straitlaced—that the vigilance committees gained their greatest renown.

And it was there that the dangers of citizens taking the law into their own hands became apparent. Although the vigilantes had wide support during most of their active period and they undoubtedly threw terror into the large and active underworld of the city, many citizens were shocked when the vigilantes broke into the jail, carried off two prisoners, and hanged them before a great crowd at the committee's headquarters, and again when they seized two other prisoners after setting up a cannon and threatening to blow open the jail.

The activities of the San Francisco vigilance committees became known throughout the West and encouraged similar groups in nearly every western state at one time or another, although most were short-lived. One of the most famous cases of vigilante action outside of San Francisco was in Montana where citizens banded together to overthrow the reign of terror of Sheriff Henry Plummer, who built up one of the most active outlaw gangs in the West.

Down in Texas, however, vigilantes became less and less necessary in enforcing the law after the Civil War. The reason was the famed Texas Rangers.

The Rangers had their beginning even before Texas independence in a group of unpaid men sent by the Spanish governor of Mexico to help defend the settlers against the Indians. In 1835 when the Texans were preparing to break away from Mexico a permanent battalion of Rangers was formed to guard the frontier.

Much of the early work of the Rangers was in protecting settlers from Indians, and during the period of the Texas Republic they gained the respect of settlers by repeated successful exploits against great odds.

During the war with Mexico that followed U. S. annexation of Texas, the reputation of the Rangers as fighting men spread through the whole country. The Civil War depleted the Ranger ranks, but after the war, in 1874, the force was reorganized in two battalions, one to work in the Indian Country to the west and the other to suppress rustling and border violations along the Rio Grande. Several times in the ensuing decades special forces of Rangers were formed to deal with dangerous gangs of bandits. Although the force had its ups and downs it has continued to the present day and the Texas Ranger remains a symbol of the taming of the Western frontier.

While the Texas Rangers were enforcing a respect for the law in many isolated towns, the Texas cowboy, far from tamed, was giving the law in Kansas some lessons in unrestrained wildness that brought to fame some of the greatest names among Western peace officers.

Texas had the cattle and the East had the money to pay for meat on the table, but between the two stood thousands of miles. Following the Civil War after the railroads pushed into Kansas, the Texans started to drive their cattle to the railheads. Thus began the famed Chisholm Trail to Abilene, Kansas. And as the fences of the grangers moved farther and farther west, blocking the great cattle drives, so did the trail towns, each in its turn becoming known as the capital of sin and violence as well as of the cattle trade. These included Ellsworth, Newton, Wichita, Caldwell, Hays, Dodge City, Ogallala, Cheyenne, Tascosa, Miles City, and Denver.

It took months to drive a herd from Texas to Abilene—months of hard, dangerous, and lonely work for the cowboys. But ahead was town. To the cowboys it meant the same as shore leave for the sailor—money in the pocket and plenty to spend it on—the gamblers, saloonkeepers, and others who flocked to the trail towns saw to that.

There were other residents of the Kansas towns, however. The section had been originally settled largely by people from the north—farmers and merchants—shrewd traders, but sternly respectable and God-fearing. They seized eagerly on the chance to profit from the cattle trade, but their hostility to the free-living Texans who brought the cattle in was undisguised. At the end of a big cattle drive the permanent population was often outnumbered by swaggering Texas cowboys, flush with money and whisky, armed and looking for their own wild brand of fun.

Many attempts were made to tame the untrammeled visitors—an ordinance was passed in Abilene prohibiting the carrying of guns, and construction of a jail was started, but the posted notices of the new ordinance had a way of becoming illegible from being riddled with bullet holes and the jail was destroyed by the cowboys before it was completed. This was the kind of situation that led the citizens to look for men of the cowboys' own type to tame them—Tom Smith and Wild Bill Hickok in Abilene, and in Dodge City, the greatest of the cow towns, a succession of the most famous gun slingers in the West—Ed and Bat Masterson, Mysterious Dave Mather, Bill Tilghman, Tom Nixon, Wyatt Earp, better known for his later exploits in Tombstone, and others.

To understand what these marshals were up against, it is helpful to get an idea of the favorite "pleasures" of the frontier.

First, there was drink. In the mining camps and cow towns, the saloon was often the first building to go up. The first bars were often simply a whisky barrel on a wagon or a board across a couple of barrels beside the trail. The drink throughout the early days of the frontier was straight whisky, drawn into a tin cup or a big tumbler right out of the barrel. This whisky was man-killing stuff, dubbed with such descriptive appelations as rotgut, red-eye, or tarantula juice. The most peaceful citizen could become a bad man when he was carrying a load of this.

As the towns grew, the saloon remained the center of social life. Its layout soon fell into the pattern that has become familiar from Western movies—the long bar, the gambling tables along the other side of the room, the large open floor space, the back rooms where private games could be conducted, and in the entrance the traditional swinging doors. The names of the saloons were indicative of the attitudes of their patrons. The Bucket of Blood was a favorite name that recurred throughout the West and there was one bluntly called the Road to Ruin. There were some saloonkeepers who tried to sound fancy with such names as Oriental Palace, but many more places were known simply as the Red Front, Blue Front, or the like.

All the saloons had gambling and the games seldom ended. Stakes were often high, sometimes running to a whole herd of cattle, and bad blood grew out of many a game. There was little or no moral stigma attached to gambling, and some of the most famous peace officers, such as Wild Bill Hickok, were inveterate gamblers.

While drinking and gambling were at the source of many a brawl which the marshals were called upon to settle, the cowboys also had more active forms of amusement that terrified the townspeople. A man who wore a pistol as naturally as he wore trousers thought nothing of sharpening his marksmanship and letting off an excess of good spirits by blazing away at street lamps, water barrels, a hat tossed in the air, or anything else that took his fancy. Furthermore, the cowboy and his horse were practically inseparable and he saw no reason why he shouldn't ride it into a saloon or a hotel. They even sometimes played poker or billiards in the saloons on horseback.

Such men could not be tamed by ordinances; the only law they respected was the law of the six-shooter backed by a man who could beat them to the draw. It is not surprising, therefore, that the gunmen selected to enforce the law were often indistinguishable from the outlaws. What is more surprising is that there were men with the courage and integrity to tame the cow towns.

While the cow towns produced some of the greatest reputations among Western peace officers, they had no monopoly on courageous law men nor on the violent conditions that tested the mettle of the staunchest gunman. Nor were all the men who brought law to the West public peace officers; many of the most successful in putting down crime were shotgun messengers on the stagecoaches, guards for the railroads and express companies, or range detectives for the cattle associations. And in addition to the men behind the badge, there was another group of men who required no less courage before there could be a stable peace on the frontier. These were the judges of the courts.

While the violence of the West is hard to exaggerate (there were some twenty thousand men of the sparse population killed in battles outside the law during the period from 1830 to the beginning of the present century), violence is, nevertheless, not the fact that stands out most strongly. In the history of every section of the western lands what impresses us most deeply is that there were always men and women who would face any odds for the principles of justice and fair play they believed in. There was a code of honor—however primitive—even among most of the outlaws and the only man truly despised was the coward.

The principles of courage, independence, and personal honor shaped in the blazing forge of frontier violence are among our most precious heritages. They provide the real meaning of the legend of the American West.

CONTENTS

xiv

CONTENTS

WESTERN SHERIFFS AND MARSHALS

1.

THE WESTERN PEACE OFFICER

As the train pulled into the lively little stopping place of Fairbank in southeastern Arizona, the express agent stood in the open door of the car, his sleeves rolled up, ready to transfer a large shipment of gold from the train to the stage for Tombstone.

A group of cowboys, playing the part of drunks, loitered around the little depot. The stage stood ready to depart, its horses pawing and snorting impatiently for the crack of the whip that would send them plunging off into a cloud of dust. A few bystanders stood casually watching the locomotive roll down the grade and grind to a stop.

Suddenly a voice shouted, "Hands up!" and the cowboys, now deadly sober, swung into ac-

tion. "All right," commanded the leader, "keep that crowd covered." Then he turned his attention to the express car.

"Throw up your hands and come down from there!"

The startled messenger stepped back and reached for a sawed-off shotgun leaning beside the door. He yelled back, "If there's something you want in here, come and get it, but be prepared to die!"

At this moment there was a shot and the agent's hat blew off as a bullet tore into the opposite side of the car. Now the bandits opened up with high-powered rifles which split the thin sides of the wooden car like paper. The express agent could not return the fire for fear of spray-

3

ing buckshot on the captives held by the bandits.

The outlaws thought they had the agent cowed and rushed to the open door of the express car. A volley of bullets cut his shirt to strips and one bullet tore through his arm, cutting an artery. The fighting agent dropped his shotgun and drew his pistol. He "threw down on" the outlaws and let go with a blast of fire that dropped one man dead in his tracks and wounded two more.

"Let's get out of here!" shouted one of the bandits. "This guy's shootin' to kill!" And get out they did as the wounded messenger finally collapsed to the floor from loss of blood.

The two principals in this fight on the evening of February 15, 1900, were both peace officers. The messenger who refused to be robbed was Jeff Davis Milton, one of the West's greatest peace officers—a deputy U.S. marshal, chief of

PAT GARRETT

JEFF MILTON

police of El Paso, and a sheriff in a dozen different counties. The leader of the determined train robbers was another peace officer—Burt Alvord, marshal of Willcox, a badman who would not hesitate to kill when the odds favored him.

All Western peace officers were gunmen of considerable standing—or they were dead men. They all relished the job—had they not they would have followed more peaceful pursuits. Some of them used their guns on the side of the law, killing only when it was necessary to perform their duty. Others were killers at heart and used their badge of office to further their own exploits and build up greater reputations as gunmen.

The job of keeping peace and order in the cow towns of the West, in the rip-roaring mining camps, and in the tough new towns that sprang up around the construction camps marking the railroads' westward path, required steel-nerved men who not only would not hesitate to draw on a killer, but who were also not afraid of being "throwed down on." In the search for peace officers who could cope with the killers

WILD BILL HICKOK

peace officer in Price, Utah, he turned in a fine record.

John Mathews was a ruthless killer before becoming sheriff of Childress County, Texas. He gave up his life fighting on the side of the law.

Bill Small was a member of the famous Hole-in-the-Wall gang of Wyoming. He left the outlaws and rustlers to become sheriff of Valley County, Wyoming, a post he filled with credit.

John Davidson roamed with outlaw bands in Texas and Oklahoma and gained the reputation of a desperate killer. He reformed and fought on the side of the law as sheriff of tough Willbarger County, Texas.

For each bad man who became a good peace officer, there was a sheriff or marshal who turned bad man. Burt Alvord was a harmless cowboy, but quick on the draw, when he became marshal of Willcox, Arizona. He immediately turned outlaw and used his badge of authority to organize a series of train robberies. After killing one of the famous Earp brothers, he left the country and went to Argentina.

and maintain some semblance of law and order, it was inevitable that bad men were often selected and given the badge of authority.

A few of the real killers turned out to be excellent peace officers. One of these was Henry Brown, who had been a noted gunman in Billy the Kid's wild gang. After Billy was killed by Sheriff Pat Garrett, Brown reformed and became a fine peace officer in Tascosa, Texas.

King Fisher had twenty-seven killings to his credit when he decided to quit being an outlaw and become a peace officer. He made a good one, too, except that he remained friends with Ben Thompson, the killer marshal of Austin, whom a lot of people were out to get. Fisher had the misfortune to be with Thompson on the night some of his enemies caught up with him, and it cost the reformed outlaw his life.

For many years Matt Warner was a handy man with a gun in the Wild Bunch which operated all over the mountain states. When the gang was about to be exterminated, Warner had to serve a prison term and reformed. Later, as a

WYATT EARP

Hendry Brown was a tough New Mexico gunman who became marshal of Caldwell, Kansas. While in office he organized a gang of outlaws who preyed upon the people he was sworn to protect. He was caught in the act of robbing a bank, and an angry mob placed a noose around his neck, ending his dual career.

Tom Horn served honorably as an Indian scout, Army officer, stock detective, and sheriff. Then he became a killer and was hanged for murder.

Ben Wheeler and Jack Sallagher had fine records before pinning on the star of marshal or sheriff, but both joined outlaw bands while in office.

Some of the most famous of all Western sheriffs and marshals were downright bad men both before and while in office. One of the most noted of these was Henry Plummer of Virginia City, Montana. Plummer organized his deputies into a gang of highwaymen. Using their knowledge of gold shipments, the sheriff's gang robbed the stages and killed indiscriminately until a vigilante committee cleaned up the whole gang with a mass hanging.

TOM SMITH

Ben Thompson, Austin's famous two-gun marshal, was a professional gambler, a killer, and a really tough character who actually provoked fights in order to add to his reputation as a bad man.

Jim Courtright's gun was for hire to the highest bidder and, while he kept the peace in Fort Worth, he was accused of showing partiality to his friends. He was finally killed by Luke Short, a gunman who also served at times as a peace officer.

Joe Beckham stole the public funds when he was sheriff of Motley County, Texas, and then shot his successor to death. His career was ended by the guns of the Texas Rangers.

Tom Gerren, while deputy sheriff of Denton County, Texas, was accused of being in league with Sam Bass, an ex-cowboy turned train robber.

Dave Mather, a gunman who served as marshal of Dodge City, Kansas, during some of the cow town's wildest days, was known as "Mysterious Dave" because he would never talk of his past. Dave was a killer both in and out of office. In one night he killed four different men in separate gun battles.

Bill Meador and John Morco were both quick on the draw and had records of killings before becoming peace officers. Meador was suspected of ridding himself of some personal enemies while wearing a marshal's star in Cuero, Texas. Morco boasted of twelve notches on his gun while marshal of Ellsworth, Kansas.

Bass Outlaw was a fearless Texas Ranger and a fine deputy U.S. marshal, but when he drank he was a killer and eventually turned bad. He was one of the notches gunman John Selman carved on his gun.

There were, however, many honest and fearless peace officers who were gunmen because only a gunman could face the killers of frontier days. Men like Billy Tilghman and Jeff Milton spent their entire adult lives fighting for law and order, and they used their guns only when it was absolutely necessary. Tom Smith seldom used a gun, depending upon his skill as a boxer to surprise and disarm his opponents.

Neil Howie of Montana and Jack Helms of

Hiram Bernard of Wyoming; Gail Hill of South Dakota; and Jim Marshall, of Colorado—all were peace officers in the finest tradition.

There were generally three classes of Western peace officers—federal, county, and city. U.S. marshals were charged with enforcing only federal laws, but they also frequently assisted in local problems. Deputy U.S. marshals often acted as sheriffs or deputies as well.

The office of sheriff was a county responsibility, while that of town marshal was a town or city function. Often the two officers, jealous of each other's reputation, refused to cooperate to keep peace and order. Frequently they even framed each other, or one officer worked secretly with the outlaws while the other tried to suppress them.

The office of town marshal was strictly a city job and his duties ended at the town limits. The marshal's job was actually often the toughest and most dangerous of the three because the marshal was exposed to the bad men and killers every day and, in some instances, every hour. At the height of the wildest days in towns like Dodge City or Abilene, a dozen or more noted gunmen could be in town at the same time and the slightest incident might touch off a gun battle. A good marshal would merely tolerate the situation; a genius was required to control it.

Good or bad, the Western peace officer—U.S. marshal, sheriff, or town marshal—was as much a part of the roaring frontier towns as the cowboys, the gunmen, the killers, the outlaws, and the other desperate men who have left their marks on the pages of Western history. It was the fearless peace officers who tamed the wildest bad men and brought law and order to replace the law of two guns and the quick draw.

Texas were men of their word and devoted themselves faithfully to preserving law and order. They could be stern and tough, but they never killed needlessly.

Chris Madsen and Heck Thomas made names for themselves as good peace officers in Oklahoma and the Indian Territory where they dealt with as many bad men as could be found in any section of the West, but they killed only in the performance of their duties. There were dozens of others: Nat Boswell, a fearless officer and a dead shot; Malcolm Campbell who had to break up a cattle war; Frank Dalton, whose four brothers followed the outlaw trail; Harry Wheeler, a noted leader of men in Arizona;

TOM SMITH

2.

TOM SMITH

THE MARSHAL WHO SELDOM USED A GUN

THE BRONZE TABLET on the four-ton red granite boulder reads:

Thomas J. Smith, Marshal of Abilene, 1870. Died a martyr to duty, Nov. 2, 1870; a fearless hero of frontier days, who in cowboy chaos established the supremacy of law.

Thus, after resting in an unmarked grave for thirty-four years, the citizens of Abilene, Kansas, paid respect to Thomas James Smith, the Irish New Yorker who in five months tamed the wildest cow town of the plains after everyone else had failed.

Tom Smith was born in New York City about 1840. After serving on the police force, some unknown tragedy or sorrow drove him west. It may have been only a love of adventure, but Tom Smith seldom talked of his past or mentioned his relatives.

In 1857 Smith showed up in Utah. He is believed to have survived the Mountain Meadows Massacre when a band of white men disguised as Indians tricked and wiped out an emigrant train. Left for dead, Tom Smith somehow managed to make his escape and for the next few years did various jobs throughout the western states. In 1868 he was working for a contracting firm building the Union Pacific Railroad across Wyoming. It was here that Tom Smith first showed the fearless stuff of which he was made.

Bear River was the town at the head of the railroad, and like all railhead towns, it was wild and woolly. While most of the young town was composed of a few hundred workers who would soon move on to the next railhead, a small group of substantial citizens planned to remain there and organized a town government. One day the town marshal arrested one of Smith's friends on a charge of drinking and locked him up in the new jail.

A short time before, three men had been

robbed and killed in the jail, and Smith feared for his friend's life. When a vigilante committee was formed, the railroad workers decided to secure their friend's release before the vigilantes' plan to hang all the jail's inmates could be carried out.

The railroad workers stormed the jail, set fire to it, and freed the prisoners. In the meantime the vigilantes barricaded themselves and opened fire on the workers. Roused to fury, Tom Smith charged the log barricade singlehanded, firing both revolvers. At last the mob was cowed, but not until Smith had received several dreadful wounds. For a time his life hung in balance.

When the Union Pacific workers moved on to the next railhead, Tom Smith was the unanimous choice for marshal. He served in this capacity in a succession of towns as the steel rails crept across Wyoming and into Utah.

When the Kansas Pacific Railroad was pushing across eastern Colorado, Tom Smith was called to keep peace and order in the rough frontier town of Kit Carson. About six feet tall and weighing around two hundred pounds, he was a powerful, athletic man, extremely quick and active. He rarely carried a gun, depending upon his strength and agility in arresting and disarming his opponents. Tom Smith believed in enforcing the law, but not in killing unless it was absolutely necessary—it seldom was.

When Kit Carson was abandoned as the railhead, Tom Smith's job was done, and he looked around for another place to tame. When Abilene, Kansas, was made the terminus of the Union Pacific Railroad, it rapidly became the wildest town of all. Tom Smith applied for the job of city marshal, but he was turned down.

In an effort to restore order in Abilene, the town officials had passed an ordinance barring the carrying of firearms. Notices to this effect were posted at the town's edges, but no sooner were they put up than the cowboys shot them full of holes.

A new jail was erected, but when the cook for one of the cowboy camps outside was locked up, the cowboys blew off the door and freed him. Then they rode through town, shooting out the street lights, and finally let Mayor Theodore Henry's house have a blast.

After several local marshals had been driven out of Abilene by the cowboys, Mayor Henry asked St. Louis to send two of its toughest policemen. They arrived at noon and headed back for St. Louis on the midnight train! Desperate, Mayor Henry wired Tom Smith to come to Abilene.

It was on a Saturday morning—a day the cowboys liked to whoop it up—in 1870 when Tom Smith walked into Mayor Henry's office. His blue-gray eyes inspired confidence and respect. He was direct and to the point when the Mayor asked him if he could handle Abilene. He said, "Give me one day to look it over."

At sundown Smith returned to Mayor Henry's office and said he would take the job. "But the pistols have got to go," he said. "An armed and drunken cowboy can be a frenzied maniac— and it looks like every cowboy in Abilene carries two guns."

Tom Smith pinned on the marshal's badge and walked off toward "Texas Abilene" south of the tracks, where the cowboys camped and

the longhorns were penned for shipment. Word swept through the camp that Abilene had a new marshal, and Big Hank, a rough bully who openly boasted that the marshal didn't live who could disarm him, strolled out to meet Smith, a pistol protruding conspicuously from his trousers.

"So you're the man who's going to run this town, eh?" Big Hank snarled when the two men met. "What do you intend to do about my gun?"

"I intend to enforce the law," replied the marshal calmly, "and I may as well start with you. Hand over your gun."

Big Hank's answer was a string of abuse. "Take it if you dare!"

Taking the bully completely by surprise,

Smith swung at the big cowboy and landed a powerful fist squarely on his chin, sending him sprawling in the dust. Disarming the bewildered Big Hank, Smith said, "You have five minutes to get out of Abilene—and don't ever let me see your face here again." Big Hank took the advice.

A prairie fire never moved faster than did the news of the new marshal's encounter through the cow camps around Abilene that night. But the cowboys weren't yet convinced, and least of all an ugly desperado called Wyoming Frank.

Taking some bets that Smith could not disarm him, Frank rode into Abilene the next morning and sent word to Smith that he was in town.

Tom Smith knew that this was the showdown. If he failed to take the gun away from Wyoming Frank he would be through. He took his time, and when he was ready he walked quietly down the middle of Abilene's dusty main street. Wyoming Frank was waiting and greeted the new marshal with a flow of insults, trying to provoke him into a quarrel and an opportunity to draw his gun.

"I'll have that gun!" Smith said, slowly approaching his man. The steel glint in Tom Smith's eyes and the determined set of his jaw told Wyoming Frank that this marshal was different from the others. Slowly he backed up, sparring for time and maneuvering for space to draw his gun, but Smith kept in close, anticipating and preventing the move.

Finally, Wyoming Frank's backward steps took him through the swinging doors of a large saloon, with Smith directly in front of him. The music stopped and the crowd gathered around the two men. "Give me your gun!" demanded the marshal, but the bully only heaped on more abuse. Then, with two flashing blows, Tom Smith lunged into the desperado and sent him crashing to the floor. In an instant the marshal had the outlaw's gun and the battle was over.

The bartender stepped from behind the bar and handed Smith his gun. "Here," he said, "take my gun. I'll not need it as long as you're marshal of this town!" The move was electric. The others stepped up and offered their guns. Tom Smith was in complete control of Abilene through a display of iron nerves.

Thus did the toughs of Abilene learn that Tom Smith was a man who meant what he said. In two days he had accomplished more in cleaning up Abilene than all the other marshals combined. In the next few months he was a familiar figure riding down the street on his gray horse Silverheels. He had little serious trouble except occasionally from a cowboy newly arrived from Texas and unaware of the marshal's reputation.

One such incident occurred one night when a big Texan, half-drunk and quarrelsome, refused to hand over his gun to Smith. Two fellow Texans grabbed pistols from behind the bar and started shooting. Someone grabbed the hanging kerosene lamp and threw it at the marshal. He dodged, got the drop on the crowd, forcibly disarmed the man, threw him over his shoulder, and carried him across the street to jail.

It was late in October and Tom Smith had been marshal of Abilene a little more than five months. He was also deputy U.S. marshal for the district and the hero of everyone except the gambling element, who felt that Smith's strict enforcement of the law was hurting their business. They planned his assassination.

Smith was lured into a room where several gunfighters were gathered. At a given signal, the lights were to be shot out and Smith would be killed by an unknown gunman. The marshal, suspicious of a trap however, drew first. When the smoke cleared, three wounded men lay on the floor and the others had stampeded. It was one of the few times Tom Smith ever drew a gun in Abilene.

Across Chapman Creek northeast of town, Andrew McConnell had killed John Shea for driving cattle across his land. The sheriff had gone out to arrest McConnell but had returned to Abilene for help. Tom Smith offered to make the arrest and, taking his deputy, Jim McDonald, with him he rode out to McConnell's farm.

McConnell and a friend, Moses Miles, were in the dark dugout McConnell used as a home. Leaving his deputy outside, Smith entered to make the arrest. Just what happened will never be known, but there was a shot and Smith, severely wounded, staggered from the dugout, pulling McConnell with him. Miles dashed out and grappled with McDonald who broke loose and fled. Miles now went to McConnell's assistance, grabbed an ax, and killed Smith.

On November 4, 1870, all Abilene suspended business while it paid homage to Tom Smith. Silverheels, his saddle empty, followed the procession to the prairie burial ground at the edge of town. Abilene had been tamed—but it would flare up again.

WILD BILL HICKOK

WILD BILL HICKOK.

3.

WILD BILL HICKOK
THE MARSHAL WHO TAMED ABILENE

OF ALL THE GUN-SLINGING SHERIFFS and marshals who fought and shot their way across the pages of American frontier history, none was more glamorous nor more controversial than Wild Bill Hickok.

Wherever Wild Bill went, his reputation as a cool, deliberate shot preceded him. Few people could feel neutral about Wild Bill. They either hated him or loved him; they either waited for a chance to kill him or were willing to be killed for him. In the end it was his reputation that cost him his life, for there were many who looked jealously upon the crown worn by Hickok and his claim to the title of the fastest man on the draw in the West.

Strangely enough, with a dozen or more noted gunmen out to get Wild Bill, the man who finally ended his colorful career was an insignificant nobody who had the reputation of being a talkative and harmless drunk.

James Butler Hickok was born on a farm in central Illinois in 1837. As a boy he learned to handle firearms, and at nineteen when he started out for the West he was already an exceptional shot.

In Kansas City the tall, blonde, blue-eyed Hickok had no trouble getting a job driving a wagon in a train of emigrants headed for the gold fields of California. After an uneventful stay in San Francisco Hickok moved on to Denver and spent the next three years hunting and trapping on the plains. Straight as a ruler, his shoulders filling out into full manhood, young Hickok was already strikingly handsome and his skill in the use of firearms was the talk of camps wherever plainsmen gathered.

In 1860 Hickok was slowly recovering from serious injuries he had received in a fight with a bear on Raton Pass in northern New Mexico. While his wounds were healing he accepted a

job with the Overland Stage Company and was sent to East Rock Creek Station in Nebraska Territory as assistant stock-tender.

East Rock Creek relay station was an important point astride the busy Oregon Trail when young Hickok arrived early in the spring of 1861, shortly after the Overland had purchased the station from David McCanles, a big powerful man and a true pioneer. Part of the purchase price had been paid in cash, the remainder to be paid off in three monthly installments. This fact was to shape the future life of James Butler Hickok, whom McCanles called "Duck Bill" because of Hickok's prominent Grecian nose. This nickname did little to endear the men to one another.

On July 1 the third and final payment on East Rock Creek Station fell due, and David McCanles wanted his money or title to the property. He rode over to see Horace Wellman, keeper of the station. Wellman had not received the money from his superiors and offered to go by wagon to Brownville on the Missouri River and bring back the money as well as a load of supplies. This was agreed to by McCanles and he asked if his twelve-year old son, Monroe, could ride along. The wagon rolled away in the dust of a hot summer day.

Twelve days later Wellman and the McCanles boy returned to find a man named Woods, McCanles' nephew, and Gordon, the McCanles hired hand, as well as Mrs. Wellman, Doc Brink, head stock-tender, and Hickok at the station. What happened in the next half-hour is still disputed, but when the smoke cleared, Woods, Gordon, and David McCanles were all dead.

In the first criminal case ever tried in Gage County, Nebraska, Hickok, Wellman, and Brink were acquitted, although Hickok admitted the shooting of McCanles. The fame of young Hickok spread far and wide, but there were those who believed at the time that Hickok was something less than a hero that tragic day at Rock Creek Station.

Leaving the West temporarily after the McCanles fight, Hickok joined the Union Army and served creditably as wagon master, sharp-

shooter, scout, and occasionally spy. He remained in service until the end of the bitter struggle and then headed again for the open plains and rough cow towns of the West.

In the two years after leaving the Union Army he was credited with the killing of Dave Tutt, a gambler, in a street duel in Springfield, Missouri. In a card game quarrel in Julesberg, Colorado, another gambler made the mistake of going for his gun, and as usual Hickok was the quicker on the draw. In Jefferson County, Missouri, he fought it out with three other opponents. All three lost, and Wild Bill's reputation as a gunman leaped to new heights. (The nickname "Bill" had stuck after the McCanles fight, and it was natural that his deeds would win him the appellation of "Wild" Bill.)

No one who knew Wild Bill Hickok was surprised when he was asked to take over the job of marshal of Hays City, Kansas, a rough frontier post teeming with scouts, cattlemen, soldiers, and desperadoes. In Hays City Wild Bill's official capacity was challenged by a gunman named Strawhan, who was in the habit of running the town to suit himself. Strawhan invited Bill out into the street, an unusual consideration for the bystanders in those days, but he went for his six-shooter a fatal second too slow. That night he was stowed away on Boot Hill with the other victims of dangerous living.

Bill Mulvey was the next desperado to question Wild Bill's authority. He was visiting in Hays City and kicking up his heels in a fashion Hickok didn't approve. When Hickok commanded Mulvey to slow down, the gunman went for his pistol. In a flash Wild Bill laid his Colt forty-five on Mulvey, who was carried out feet first.

To complicate further Wild Bill's task of keeping peace in Hays City, the U.S. Seventh Cavalry moved into the area in 1870 and many of the soldiers felt immune to Hickok's deadly rule. Trouble reached a climax one night when a big sergeant got out of hand in Paddy Welch's place on the town's main street.

Called in to restore order, Wild Bill soon found himself in a rough-and-tumble brawl with some fourteen tough and hardened troopers of General Phil Sheridan's command. From all accounts, Hickok was unarmed when the

fight started, but his friend Paddy managed somehow to get a gun to him through the maze of flying arms and legs. In the crush, Hickok managed to fire the gun just once, and the bullet killed a young officer.

Severely wounded, Wild Bill left Hays City before the Army could retaliate, and he was well on his way east on a fast horse when General Sheridan sent a cavalry detachment in pursuit with orders to bring back the marshal dead or alive. Exercising the discretion that had prolonged his life several times, Wild Bill left Kansas and did not return until the Seventh Cavalry had pulled out for the Sioux country to the north.

Just before his return, polite, soft-spoken, and courageous Tom Smith had given up his life enforcing the deadly weapon ordinance as marshal of Abilene. Now Abilene was looking for a new marshal, and Wild Bill was by this time the best-known gunman west of the Missouri.

When Hickok took over as marshal of Abilene his feats with revolvers were almost fabulous. He could dent a tossed coin with a bullet in mid-air. With a pistol in each hand he could keep a tomato can dancing in the dust. He could perforate a hat brim while it was spinning in the air. And while marshal of Abilene he killed two gunmen, who were fleeing in opposite directions, so rapidly that a witness swore at the inquest that only one shot had been fired.

The new marshal was as colorful in his dress as in his fighting. He wore the shoulder-length hair popular with plainsmen and buffalo hunters. It was silken and curly, and with the fancy dress—Prince Albert coat, checkered trousers, embroidered silk waistcoat, fine boots, and wide-brimmed black hat—he was an unforgettable character.

One of Wild Bill's first acts of public improvement in Abilene was the killing of the gambler, Phil Coe, a tall bearded Texan, who, like all of the Texans who brought their herds to Abilene, resented the marshal's iron rule. Standing less than eight feet apart on Abilene's main street, Wild Bill and Phil Coe shot it out point-blank. Finally Coe went down, and Wild Bill finished him off just as his deputy and good friend, Mike

Williams, came running up, revolver drawn, to see what the shooting was all about. Believing the approaching man to be a Texan coming to Coe's aid, Hickok spun and fired, killing his best friend.

In a personal encounter, Wild Bill later killed Phil Coe's cousin in Wichita. He also killed a cattleman in an Ellsworth, Kansas, restaurant. The real tally of his killings, however, has long been lost. Some say it was 50; others claim it approached 100.

By 1872, Wild Bill Hickok had brought a semblance of law and order to Abilene, but conditions were changing. No longer were the great herds of bawling longhorns coming to the railhead on the plains, and the fun-loving Texas cowboys were becoming fewer each year. Wild Bill no longer found in Abilene scope for his talents with twin double-action Army pistols. He left Abilene to its memories and joined the Army as a civilian scout in the Indian country.

Still in his thirties, Wild Bill was a national figure, a hero or a killer depending upon one's view. In 1874 he joined one of Ned Buntline's traveling shows which toured the country east of the Mississippi. In his act Hickok was to kill a number of Indians by firing blanks at them. Bored with the act, Wild Bill wished to end the contract, but the other actors protested that it would break up the show. In St. Louis, Hickok blistered the thighs of the "dead" Indians with hot wads from his smoking guns until they jumped up and ran for the river with Wild Bill in pursuit. Hickok was released from his contract.

In April 1876, Wild Bill joined the gold rush to Deadwood in the Black Hills, where he did a little prospecting and considerable poker playing at the Number Ten with old friends. Many people sought his company, including the noted gunmen of the day, but Wild Bill knew that most of them would be willing to kill him for the glory of inheriting his six-shooter championship.

On the afternoon of August 2, 1876, he entered the Number Ten to join Carl Mann, one of the owners, a Missouri River boat pilot named Captain Frank Massey, and Charley Rich, a professional gambler and gunman. The three men were already seated at Hickok's favorite table, and Rich was occupying Wild Bill's usual chair—the one with its back to the wall, a precaution that Hickok had practiced throughout his life. Wild Bill objected mildly, but as a joke, Rich made the ex-peace officer take the seat with its back to the bar.

The game was proceeding quietly and the players hardly noticed Jack McCall, a drunken, cross-eyed tinhorn gambler, enter the saloon. McCall stumbled over to the bar, ordered a drink, downed it in one gulp, and, wiping his scraggly mustache with his sleeve, ambled toward the door. This move took him to within two feet of the back of Wild Bill's chair. At this point he swung about, suddenly producing a Colt forty-five. Pointing the gun squarely at Hickok's head, McCall fired once, and the man who tamed Abilene slumped forward, his cards slowly falling from his hand—aces and eights which gamblers still know as the "Deadman's Hand."

Captured and tried, McCall was acquitted on the strength of his story that Wild Bill had once killed one of his relatives. A few weeks later, however, in a Cheyenne saloon, McCall got drunk and was overheard by a deputy U.S. marshal boasting that he had no real reason for killing Wild Bill. He was arrested, retried, and hanged for killing the king of the gunmen.

The percentages of a gunman's life caught up with James Butler Hickok in his thirty-ninth year, but of all the professional gunmen who would have killed Wild Bill for fancied or real purposes, the man who finally accomplished it was far from a professional. In the cylinder of his Colt forty-five were found five loaded chambers and one empty. Every professional gunman in Wild Bill's time always had one empty chamber in a gun's cylinder for safety purposes. If Jack McCall had followed that practice and discarded the bullet that killed Wild Bill Hickok, the marshal of Abilene might have lived out a full life—because the other five bullets were all dead.

TOM ALLEN

4.

TOM ALLEN

THE MARSHAL WHO USED HIS FISTS INSTEAD OF HIS GUN

Tom Allen lived as rough a life as any peace officer, but he ended his days without being wounded, without killing a man, and without being backed down in a fight. He never made a threat or a promise that he did not keep. He never sought a fight, but he never avoided one either.

Tom Allen was born in Ireland of well-to-do parents who named him Thomas Allen Cullinan. In Junction City, Kansas, where he made his name as a peace officer of the finest type, he was seldom known by any other name than Tom Allen.

Tom loved adventure and wanted to see the world. At the age of eleven he left his comfortable home in Kilrush, County Clare, to go to sea. For three years in the revenue service he served along the coasts of France and the British Isles

and in the Mediterranean. Then came trips to Germany, the Indies, South America, the Crimea, and all the great parts of the world. In 1855, he signed on a passenger ship running between Liverpool and New York. On the second voyage to this country he decided to stay.

Soon tiring of the city, Allen went west and shipped out as a seaman on a Great Lakes boat. After a year or so of this and one shipwreck in Lake Erie, he moved on to further adventures on the Mississippi River.

Although he had only been in the United States a short time, he had become a citizen and he was extremely proud of his adopted land. On a raft of logs going down the Mississippi, he was with a gang of foreign-born men who were abusing the United States. Allen listened as long as he could stand it and then asked each man in turn if he had become a United States citizen. Not one had bothered to take out his first papers. In no uncertain terms, Tom Allen notified the foreigners to go back to their own land if they didn't like the United States.

After working his way up to be river pilot, Tom Allen quit in 1857 and went to Kansas. There he hired out to the American Fur Company and ranged the Rocky Mountains from Yellowstone to Taos, hunting and trapping.

determination to defend his rights won out. All he did was to threaten to open fire and fight to the death if the men advanced a step farther. The small army retreated without firing a shot.

The claim did not work out and before long Tom Allen moved on to new adventures. He worked in the mines around Colorado where he became known as "Yellow Tom" from the buckskin suit that he habitually wore painted with yellow ochre.

During the summer of 1858, he stayed on the enormous New Mexico ranch of Lucian Maxwell, who was one of the largest landholders in the West. Here Allen met and made friends with the famous scout and frontiersman, Kit Carson, who had a small interest in the Maxwell ranch. Near fall when Tom Allen was ready to travel on, Kit offered him five hundred head of cattle as an inducement to stay. But adventure was part of Tom Allen's makeup. He traveled on.

In the fall of 1858 Allen and two companions built a log cabin on a ninety-acre claim near the present site of Denver. The ownership of the land was contested, and for protection the men made a fort of the cabin, with portholes from which they could defend themselves. Eighty armed men arrived to drive the three men off, but Tom Allen's steel nerve and his stubborn

A defender of women, Allen once happened upon a bully slapping a woman in Denver. When Allen intervened, the would-be bad man turned upon Allen and the two men squared off. The fight lasted one hour and twenty minutes, but Tom Allen did not quit until his opponent agreed never to commit the offense again.

A master of the rough-and-tumble style of fighting, Tom Allen preferred it to the use of his gun because no one got killed. Once he caught a character known as the "Terror of the Gulch" stealing his sluice water. Allen tried to reason with the man, but to no avail. When the Terror pulled his gun, Allen knocked it from his hand instead of drawing his own gun and shooting the man. In the brutal fight that followed, Tom beat his man into submission.

In the summer of 1860, Allen and two companions set off on an exploration trip to the Colorado River country and were captured by the Ute Indians. The Utes were not abusive, but were careful that their prizes did not escape. One day one of the Indian warriors insisted upon pulling Tom's ear. Allen got tired of the fun and, after warning the Indian to stay away, knocked him down. This brought about a conference with the chief, during which Tom argued that the prairie Indians were far superior to the mountain Indians in hand-to-hand battle, but that he, Tom Allen, could lick any single Indian living. The chief disagreed with this and arranged a fight between Tom and the strongest Ute warrior. Tom whipped the big Indian so impressively that the amazed chief released his captives immediately.

At the outbreak of the Civil War, Tom returned to Kansas and enlisted as an Indian scout, serving throughout the western states. He was in Leavenworth, Kansas, in 1863 when the town was taken over by a band of ruffians. The police were overpowered, the city marshal was driven out of town, and two officers were killed. Tom Allen was urged to become marshal. He did so and in thirty days he had cleaned up the gangs and restored order. Then he resigned.

After the war, he went to Fort Laramie, Wyoming, but soon returned east to Junction City,

Kansas, as a partner in a business to supply beef to the soldiers stationed at near-by Fort Riley, one of the Army's main western outposts. At the same time his firm supplied meat to the construction gangs building the M K & T Railroad across the plains into Texas and Oklahoma. This job kept him pretty much on the move.

In the fall of 1871, Tom settled down in Junction City. It was not long before he was elected city marshal, a job he held until his death, with the exception of a couple of years spent in Kansas City.

One of the big problems of policing Junction City was the handling of the soldiers from Fort Riley. On one occasion he singlehandedly arrested and locked up eight soldiers after subduing them in a free-for-all fight. To Tom Allen, it was unthinkable to pull a gun, although to have done so would have saved him much suffering. He would not risk killing a man to make an arrest, and in all of his years of service as Marshal of Junction City, he never had a killing laid to his hand.

One day a tough new recruit came to Junction City with thirteen soldiers, all determined to teach the marshal a lesson once and for all. They jumped Tom in a saloon. In the brawl, which wrecked the place, Allen knocked out seven of the soldiers and dragged them off to the town jail. The others were glad to flee for their lives.

Tom Allen's reputation as a fighter with his fists was known far and wide, but there was always some tough to challenge the marshal in spite of his ability to take care of himself. A big six-foot bully arrived in town one day in 1884 and boasted that he was going to run the marshal out of town. Tom knew the man was plenty tough and a fighter with a reputation of his own.

When the two men met, the newcomer picked a quarrel and Tom ordered him to leave town.

"Who's going to make me?" roared the bully.

"There's a train leaving in thirty minutes," Tom replied calmly. "I want you to be on it." Allen walked away.

When the train pulled out without the bad man, Tom found him getting drunk in a near-by saloon. "Now, I'm going to take you in," Tom said. "Come along."

"You're not man enough to take me in," sneered the bad man, slapping Tom in the face. With one blow the marshal felled the bully, disarmed him, and dragged him off to jail. He was on the next train out.

Serving also as a deputy U.S. marshal, Tom was once called upon to serve an arrest warrant upon himself. He had purchased some articles from a soldier, which proved to have been stolen. A disgruntled soldier filed a complaint against Tom, and the U.S. marshal sent Tom the warrant to serve on himself. Tom did so and appeared in court to defend the charge. He was acquitted in seven minutes—the only time in his long career that a complaint was brought against him.

By unanimous consent of all the citizens of Junction City, Tom Allen served his community from 1871 to 1904 with the exception of two years. He reported to eighteen different mayors, each of whom trusted him to handle all police matters in his own manner. He was the law unto himself and he preserved order without abusing his authority. Thomas Allen Cullinan was a rare peace officer. When he died on June 18, 1904, every man, woman, and youngster in Junction City mourned for the man with the wonderful power and judgment to restrain himself when other men were quick to kill.

BILL TILGHMAN

5.

BILL TILGHMAN

FIFTY YEARS A PEACE OFFICER

WILLIAM MATTHEW TILGHMAN was a quiet, soft-spoken man who never drank, smoked, or used abusive language—yet for fifty years he served as one of the greatest peace officers of the frontier West.

Billy Tilghman was born in Fort Dodge, Iowa, on the Fourth of July in 1849. While he was still a small child, his parents moved to a farm near Atchison, Kansas. When he was eight, his father marched away to the Civil War and Billy had to become the man of the family.

At fourteen Billy was a tall, wiry lad, and already a crack shot with pistol or rifle, an expert swimmer, and an unrivaled horseman. He hired out as a stock herder and soon was doing all kinds of jobs. In 1870 he made a trip to the plains of western Kansas where buffalo roamed so thick they covered the prairies like a blanket for miles. The life of a buffalo hunter appealed

to Bill, and by the following year he had become a full-fledged hunter. Before long he and a friend secured a contract to supply meat to a contractor who was building the Atchison, Topeka and Santa Fe Railroad through the country.

Hunting was a rough and dangerous life. Indians still roamed the country and frequently attacked with unpredictable suddenness. The plains were full of bandits and all those tough characters who felt safer where there was a minimum of law and order. A man lived by his gun, and young Bill Tilghman had learned to hold his own with the best gunmen the country could offer. Altogether Bill managed to account for 7500 buffalo with his own gun.

Bill drifted into Colorado, hunting and trading with the Indians, most of whom respected him for his honesty and the consideration with

which he treated them. In the Indian Territory Bill got to know several famous chiefs.

In 1874 Bill and his party tried some hunting in the Panhandle section of northern Texas. They were soon forced to leave the area, however, because of the increasing hostility and treachery of the Indians, who were making a last-ditch attempt to drive the white hunters from their sacred buffalo grounds. Bill missed the famous battle at Adobe Walls by three days.

Because of his knowledge of the Indian country and his ability to get along with most of the red men, young Bill Tilghman was sworn in as a deputy sheriff by Sheriff Charlie Bassett of Ford County, Kansas, and sent out to recover a herd of stolen oxen from their Indian captors. It was his first peace officer commission and he completed the job singlehanded. From that time to the end of his long, full career, Bill Tilghman was seldom without the badge of authority pinned to his vest.

When the famous Bat Masterson was elected sheriff of Ford County, he selected Bill Tilghman as his deputy. Now Bill's plainsman's life was over. It was January 1878, and forty-six years of law enforcement were ahead of the strong, blue-eyed young man from Iowa. He had roughed it over the whole Western frontier. He knew every stream, every trail, and every rock in six states. He knew every trick of surviving in a country where life was cheap.

As deputy sheriff of Ford County, Bill's headquarters were in Dodge City, that explosive cow town which attracted the wildest cowboys and the deadliest gunners, professional gamblers, scouts, traders, and men of prey of all types. Shooting up the town was a traditional sport and dead lawmen were commonplace.

His duties were largely in the office, keeping records, feeding the prisoners, and running the jail, but he took up his work with a determination to make good. He studied the habits of bad men as he had studied the ways of the buffalo as a boy. There is no telling how many times Billy Tilghman's keen insight into the ways of bad men saved his life in later years.

After Masterson's two-year term was up, Bill left Dodge City, scouted for awhile with the Army, and worked on a railroad that was being built in New Mexico. After a little more than a year he returned to Dodge City and became deputy again under Sheriff Pat Sughrue.

Together, Sughrue and Tilghman spared no effort in tracking down a wanted man. Once they rode more than one hundred miles in twenty hours, and on another occasion Billy traveled over two thousand miles to make an arrest. Of course, when Sughrue's two-year term was up, Bill was again out of a job, but he had taken up a small claim near Dodge City and was slowly stocking it with cattle.

Billy Tilghman was too good a law officer to be left to the peaceful life of a cattleman. He was offered the job of city marshal and accepted, pinning on the badge made from a twenty-dollar gold piece. It was April 1884, and Dodge City was bursting its sides as the tide of Texas longhorns streamed in from the trails, bringing with them thousands of thirsty cowboys eager for a wild night on the town.

One day "Mysterious Dave" Mather—no one knew much about him except that he was mighty handy with a gun—killed Bill's deputy, Tom Nixon. Bill Tilghman got the drop on Mysterious Dave and disarmed him. This hurt Dave's pride and he swore to kill the marshal. He was known to be a man of his word.

Mysterious Dave left Dodge City, but he soon returned, loaded down with pistols, rifles, shotguns, and plenty of ammunition. He moved his arsenal into an upstairs room of a lodging house overlooking the main street. From his window he planned to drop Bill Tilghman in his tracks, but Mysterious Dave had trapped himself. The only entrance to his room was by an outside stairway. All Tilghman had to do was place a guard at the stairs with instructions to arrest Dave when he came out. The outlaw remained inside for a week and then surrendered. He left town and was never seen there again.

Billy Tilghman had a knack of controlling bad men without killing them, unlike many of his fellow peace officers. Although his handling of the wild and reckless crowd of Dodge City was not a display of his prowess with a six-shooter, it was nonetheless effective. He hated killings and took dangerous risks to prevent them. Certain of his quickness and accuracy, he waited until the last split second before drawing his own gun. When he fired, he never missed. When troublemakers heard the ring of his commanding voice, they obeyed. He tried to head off trouble before it started, and he kept peace in Dodge City so effectively that his reputation was talked about from Canada to Mexico.

After two years Bill resigned as marshal and again turned to ranching. Hard times had come to the plains, however, and after a few years he sold out and went to Oklahoma, taking up a claim near Chandler. Bill had hardly settled in the new country when the U.S. marshal selected him as a deputy. Bill dropped his farming and began his service for the government which lasted twenty-one years. His territory covered what is now the state of Oklahoma with frequent trips into other states to round up a desperado or recover stolen stock.

Since the wilds of Oklahoma often baffled pursuit, it was full of desperate men from all walks of life, including members of the Dalton gang and the reckless killers of the Doolin band. Bill Doolin was a lanky, illiterate man. He had once ridden with the Daltons, but later he organized his own gang. He knew every hideout in the country and holed up in one near the little town of Ingalls where there was always a guard to warn of the approach of an officer.

Bill Tilghman was assigned to go out and bring in Bill Doolin. He had known Doolin as a hard-riding cowboy and had frequently befriended him. He wanted to take him alive if possible, but dead if he must.

His deputies were two fearless men who later became famous in their own right—Heck Thomas and Chris Madsen. Their chase continued for months, but the slippery outlaw seemed to lead a charmed life and escaped from trap after trap. In 1896 the trail led Tilghman to Eureka Springs, Arkansas, where the outlaw was hiding in a rooming house. Tilghman was alone, his deputies far behind, running down another trail.

The capture of Bill Doolin singlehanded was considered an impossible feat, but Billy Tilghman pulled it off. He simply met Doolin unexpectedly in a bathhouse and ordered him to throw up his hands. As Doolin hesitated, Billy commanded, "Bill, I don't want to kill you but if you move one inch closer to that gun, I'll end your career right here!"

For all of Bill Tilghman's brave work, Doolin was soon free again. He escaped from the Federal penitentiary at Guthrie and had a few months of freedom before being blasted by the quick-shooting Heck Thomas.

In 1900 Bill Tilghman was elected sheriff of Lincoln County, Oklahoma, and re-elected two years later. By this time the old outlaw gangs had been exterminated or broken up. Yet there were numerous bank robberies, horse stealings and cattle rustling crimes to keep Bill busy.

In 1911 the city commissioners of Oklahoma City asked Tilghman to be their chief of police. The old peace officer sold his ranch and cattle and moved to the city. After two years of hard work, however, he resigned, in poor health.

In 1915, as an authority on the outlaw gangs of the West, Bill was hired to supervise the production of a motion picture of outlaw life. For a few years he helped promote the film.

Then in 1924 the oil boom came to the little town of Cromwell, west of Oklahoma City. It was a boom town with all the rough and wild characteristics of the early frontier towns with which the old peace officer was so familiar. When the call came to Bill to take over as chief of police, he could not resist and once more he pinned on the badge of authority.

The single-street town of Cromwell was full of modern criminals who, unlike those of the Old West, completely lacked a sense of honor. In a way they were even more dangerous than the most noted killers of the frontier.

On November 1, 1924, after being on duty in Cromwell only a few months, Bill Tilghman was having a cup of coffee in a restaurant when he heard a shot outside. He rushed out to investigate and walked squarely into a drink-crazed man (who turned out to be a prohibition officer on a spree) brandishing a revolver. Two shots were fired and Bill's fifty years of service on the side of the law came to a sudden and tragic end.

BAT MASTERSON

6.

BAT MASTERSON

THE DANDY OF DODGE CITY

MOST KILLERS of the old West enjoyed their notorious reputations, even killing deliberately to add another notch to their gun. Notches were recognized as a kind of badge of distinction among certain gentry of the rough-and-ready frontier towns, and to knock off a noted gunman was in effect to add his notches to your own, whether you were outlaw or peace officer.

Bat Masterson was different. He did not enjoy the name "killer," though it was tacked on to him. Unlike the cold, calculating gunman of Western fiction and in real life, he preferred to be known as a good guy who liked a joke.

By very nature, Bat was a genial, lovable character, extremely loyal to his friends and a lover of practical pranks, even when played at his expense. In his younger days, he was a foppish dresser—a dandy without a care in the world. He drifted into being a peace officer—and made a very good one.

William Barclay Masterson was still a small child when his parents followed the path westward from Illinois. They settled in Kansas, which was then Indian country and where the red men were fiercely resisting the destruction of their vast buffalo herds.

Life on the frontier was rugged and rough. Schools as such did not exist, and law was a thing a man made for himself at the point of a gun. Boys grew into men at an early age and handled a pistol along with their elders as a part of everyday life. It was just the kind of a world that appealed to Bat and his younger brother Ed.

Hunter, scout, trading-post owner, gambler, restaurant worker, faro dealer—Bat went through the usual course of the day, taking whatever work he could find, making friends wherever he went. He was eighteen, but a mature man, when he arrived in Dodge City, the self-acclaimed "cow capital of the world" and the toughest town this side of Hell.

Young Bat saw a chance to make a fortune in buffalo hunting and, with another chap, secured a contract to supply meat for the construction crews of the Santa Fe Railroad. Everything went fine until Bat's partner skipped out with the profits. Bat laughed the matter off and charged it up to experience.

In 1874, he was with a band of trappers and hunters at Adobe Walls, in the Texas Panhandle, when they were attacked by hundreds of Kiowa Indians. Of the twenty-eight men and lone woman, Bat Masterson was the youngest, but when the siege had ended, no man could lay down his rifle with more satisfaction than the kid from Dodge City. He was a hero.

After the Battle of Adobe Walls, Bat returned to Dodge City, which was bursting at the sides with hundreds of wild and reckless cowboys, fresh in from the trails, their pockets loaded with money and their hearts set on a wild and woolly spree. Wild Bill Hickok was sheriff and doing a pretty fair job of riding herd on the cowboys— but he could always use another good deputy. He hired Bat Masterson, and the two men became close friends.

When Wild Bill tired of Dodge City and moved on to greener pastures, Bat was elected sheriff and his brother Ed was made deputy marshal. Although Bat was hardly old enough to vote, Dodge had faith in him. He did not attempt to enforce blue laws upon the cowboys who flooded into Dodge. If they behaved themselves without shooting up the town, the new sheriff permitted them to have their fun—and even joined them.

Many of the cowboys from Texas were ex-Confederate soldiers who were none too happy about the outcome of the Civil War. They wel-

comed every chance to tangle with a Yankee. To prevent gunfire, Bat enforced the anti-gun-carrying ordinance and had less trouble with this crime-prevention law than any of his predecessors or immediate followers. It was a mean character, indeed, who could resist Bat's pleasant reminder to "check your pistols with the bartender."

Bat was not the type to look for trouble, but neither would he turn his back to it if the situation justified action. He made more friends than enemies—a rare accomplishment for a peace officer in early Dodge City or any other town of its caliber.

Clay Allison, a Texan with a great reputation as a gunman, arrived in Dodge City while Bat was in office and announced that he was out to get himself a Yankee sheriff. Being the peace-loving man that he was, Bat didn't rush out to greet Allison, but let things take their course.

Allison was accompanied by a group of staunch supporters, and they headed immediately for the bars to get in shape for the fun. They had so much fun that they completely forgot about Clay's mission and rode back to camp that night whooping it up and filling the night with reckless gun shots. Bat stood by ready to swing into action if the party got out of hand, but for the life of him, he couldn't see why he should step into that wild mob and get his head shot off.

Bat had a persuasive way with the most hardened gunmen, and he left the job of killing them off to others. Ben Thompson, the bad-man peace officer from Texas, had the obnoxious habit of shooting at people just for the fun of it when he was drinking. One night he decided to

go backstage at the local theater and pick off an actor or two. Bat was watching for trouble and followed the big Texan. Just as Thompson was drawing on the leading character, Bat stepped up and knocked the gun from his hand. Thompson raged in fury.

"Don't be a fool, Ben," the sheriff cautioned. "Somebody'll sure kill you before you get off of this stage if you harm these people! After the show we'll have a shooting match to see who can shoot out the most lights!"

Thompson was so taken aback at this new approach that he stormed out of the theater, roaring with laughter. Both he and the sheriff lived another day because of Bat's big heart. Later on, Bat Masterson saved the life of Ben Thompson's younger brother, Billy, when he was about to be torn apart by a mob. It wasn't that Billy was worthy of saving—he was a ruthless killer—it was just that Bat Masterson believed in living and letting live.

If Bat ever lost his temper, it was when someone tried to take advantage of his kid brother Ed, who was serving Dodge City as deputy town marshal. On his routine tour of duty one night Ed walked into the Lone Star Dance Hall just as Bob Shaw, a liquored-up cowboy, was about to send Texas Dick to eternity. Ed lacked his brother's grand sense of humor and proceeded to settle the matter in a businesslike fashion. As he drew his gun, Shaw shot him in the chest. Ed went down fighting, flipping his pistol to his uninjured arm and winging the drunken cowboy in the arm and leg. As Ed lay on the floor in pain, he held the Texans at bay until help arrived. Then and there Bat swore that the next man who laid a gun on brother Ed would have to pay with his life.

That day came five months later when Ed walked into a saloon and attempted to disarm two noisy and gun-brandishing Texans, Al Walker and Fred Wagner by name. Without warning and before Ed had a chance to draw, they shot him down. Bat arrived a moment later. He covered the crowd while he held his dying brother in his arms and, seeing the guns still smoking in Walker's and Wagner's hands, he went completely mad. As Bat carried out the body of his brother, other men dragged out Walker and Wagner by the heels, both dead.

After Dodge City began to tame down, most of its notorious characters—good and bad—moved on to Tombstone, Arizona, where life was still wild and free and one could hear the crack of guns in the night. Many of his old friends were there—Wyatt Earp, Luke Short, Charlie Bassett, and others. Some of these men were on the side of the law, others were not, but that didn't matter to Bat Masterson if the man was in trouble and needed his help. Time and time again he endangered his own life to save a friend, who was often not worthy of the risk.

Tiring of Tombstone and the years of frontier warfare, Bat went to Denver and there he took up dealing cards in a gambling casino. He became a city favorite and a walking encyclopedia of the West. Ask him who had fired first in such and such a fray, and Bat could fill in all the details. Who was with Luke Short when he killed Charlie Storms? Bat could describe the shirt Charlie wore and the way he slumped to the floor, smoking pistol still clutched tight.

Bat made Denver his home for many years but occasionally he strolled away to recapture

some of the flavor of the roaring days long gone by. When President Theodore Roosevelt offered him the job of U.S. marshal in the Indian Territory (Oklahoma), Bat declined, saying thoughtfully: "The job is not for me. Oklahoma is still wild and woolly and there is always some ambitious young kid who would want to shoot it out with me to see how good the old man really was. I would have to kill or be killed, and I have taken my guns off for the last time."

Instead, Masterson accepted a deputy U.S. marshal's appointment in New York where guns had ceased to roar when the West was still young. Always interested in athletics of all kinds, it gave him an opportunity to see baseball and boxing matches. Eventually he became a sports writer for one of the New York newspapers. He was sitting at his desk on October 25, 1921, a sheet of paper before him upon which he had just written —"Everybody gets about the same amount of ice during his lifetime. The rich get their in summer time, and the poor in winter."

With these words Bat Masterson, the dandy of Dodge City, the gunman who hated to kill, the peace officer who outfaced Ben Thompson, slumped over dead.

JIM COURTRIGHT

7.

JIM COURTRIGHT

THE MARSHAL WHO CAME BACK

JIM COURTRIGHT was the first city marshal of Fort Worth, Texas, to serve more than one term. The job required an ice-nerved gunman, one who could inspire confidence and loyalty in his deputies and who could keep the notorious gunmen of his day in check. That man was Jim Courtright, who was completely ignorant of the word "fear."

A tall, dark-skinned man, Courtright sometimes let his hair grow to his shoulders, a custom common among gunmen and Indian scouts. Around his waist were strapped two six-shooters, butts forward, but unlike most two-gun slingers, he did not use the crossbow style of drawing them. Courtright claimed it was faster to draw the right gun with the right hand and the left with the left, and he proved more than once that he was right.

As marshal of Fort Worth from 1876 through 1879, his reputation for speed on the draw and for unerring accuracy was well known around Texas, and few men rose to challenge him. He relentlessly pursued murderers, train robbers, rustlers, and horse thieves, but many people criticized Courtright's friendly attitude toward the gamblers of Fort Worth. He often gambled himself, and as long as the gamblers were not unruly, he protected them—they were his friends. In the end, however, it was a gambler who killed him, and a former friend at that—the only man who ever beat him to the draw.

Born in Iowa about 1848, Jim Courtright served as a scout and trooper on the Union side during the Civil War. After the war he came to Texas and soon had earned reputation enough as a gunman to get the city marshal job at Fort Worth.

His real name was Tim, but somehow he became known as Jim and, because of his long hair, he was frequently known as Long Hair Jim. On Saturday nights during the trail season Fort Worth was a wild town with hundreds of cowboys on the loose for a good time. It was not unusual for Courtright to arrest twenty-five or thirty cowboys over the weekend. Once a reckless cowboy had been "handled" by big Jim Courtright he usually stayed on his good behavior while in Fort Worth.

After serving out his second term as Fort Worth's city marshal, Courtright went to Lake Valley, New Mexico, a wild, rip-roaring mining camp where he had been recommended for the marshal's job. His deputy was Jim McIntyre, himself handy with a gun.

Lake Valley had grown up around the silver mines of the American Mining Company, and one of Courtright's main jobs was to protect the ore trains with their valuable cargoes. One night a group of bandits made the mistake of trying to rob one of the ore trains right under Courtright's nose. McIntyre and Courtright killed two of the robbers and pushed the train through to its destination. There was some talk at the time that the bandits were needlessly killed and could have been captured instead.

Soon after Courtright had tamed Lake Valley, the ore played out and the camp closed down, leaving Courtright out of a job. He located in the American Valley as ranch foreman for General Logan, but actually his job consisted of cleaning up the rustlers of the region and discouraging the squatters who were attempting to farm the grazing lands which were public property but considered by many cattlemen to be their own.

McIntyre followed Courtright to the Logan ranch, where he was hired through Courtright's influence. The two Texans attempted to move a group of squatters from Logan's range, and in the fight that followed two squatters were killed. The New Mexico authorities charged Courtright and McIntyre with murder and reopened the case of the killing of the bandits at Lake Valley. Courtright and McIntyre fled, claiming they would not have had a fair trial.

Back in Fort Worth, Courtright opened a private detective agency. During the great railroad strike of 1886 Courtright was placed in charge of the armed guards to ride the trains through town. On one occasion a band of strikers and sympathizers attacked an outbound train at the edge of town and in the hot and furious gun battle that followed, several strikers were wounded and one of the guards was killed. The strike was settled, but many people were angered with Courtright's part as a railroad guard. Yet he continued to have many friends and remained a popular figure in Fort Worth, highly respected for his skill as a gunman.

One day three men stepped from an eastbound train and looked up Courtright for what appeared to be a friendly chat. Two of the men were Texas Rangers; the third was Captain Harry Richmond, Chief of Police of Albuquerque, New Mexico. That evening Jim spent considerable time with the three visitors, going from bar to bar and looking up old friends.

On the following morning Courtright was invited to the hotel where the three men were staying in a second-floor room. The ostensible purpose of the visit was to look at some pictures of wanted criminals. Although New Mexico had repeatedly tried to extradite Courtright and McIntyre from Texas, the Texas governor had consistently refused to sign the papers. Courtright, thus, felt rather secure in Fort Worth but, just in case there should be trouble, he took with him an old friend, Deputy Sheriff Jim Maddox. At the hotel, however, Maddox was delayed in the lobby and Courtright went upstairs alone.

Courtright thumbed through many pictures with the three visitors and, believing everything to be on the level, relaxed his guard. Suddenly he looked up to find all three men covering him with revolvers. He was immediately placed in chains and informed that he was under arrest for murder in New Mexico. Chief of Police Richmond produced the extradition papers which the Texas governor had secretly signed. Courtright was told that he would be held in the hotel until the nine o'clock train left for Albuquerque that evening.

In the meantime, Courtright's friend, Maddox, tired of waiting and went home. All day long Courtright was kept under guard in the hotel room and, as it was his habit to sleep most of the day, his absence around town was not noticed.

At eight o'clock, just as the officers were preparing to sneak Courtright to the near-by depot, a train pulled in from the west and someone stepped off with the news that Jim McIntyre had been arrested by New Mexico officials in Wichita Falls. This immediately created some curiosity as to Courtright's whereabouts and it was soon learned that he was under arrest and being held a prisoner in the hotel.

A crowd immediately gathered in the streets and shouted demands for their friend's release. Sensing that the mob might attempt to force their prisoner's release, the officials secretly took Courtright out a back entrance and whisked him into a waiting carriage. It took off at a gallop for the Fort Worth jail, but the mob immediately spotted it and gave chase.

Fearing the mob might release Courtright during the trip to the depot, it was decided to hold Courtright in jail until the short trip could be safely made. He was not locked in a cell, but kept under heavy guard. He was taken to a near-by restaurant for meals, and here the escape plan was put to work.

While the guards were pushing their prisoner past the crowd jamming the street outside the restaurant, someone brushed Courtright and managed to whisper a message to him. It was the evening meal and the restaurant was crowded, but a special table was ready for the officials and their famous prisoner.

During the course of the meal, Courtright dropped his napkin and, turning to the guard next to him, said, "Will you pick it up?"

"Pick it up yourself," snapped the guard, continuing with his meal. "Do you think I'm your servant?"

Courtright stooped to recover the napkin from beneath the table. Then he rose quickly to

his feet, shoved back his chair, and covered the amazed guards with a pistol in each hand.

"Stand back now and no one will get hurt!" Courtright shouted. "You had your trick; now it's my turn!"

Aware of Courtright's reputation and accuracy, none of the guards made a move. The crowd surged in, leaving a path to the door, and Courtright backed out to a saddled horse waiting at the curb. Firing both pistols, he rode away while the crowd shouted its approval.

That night Courtright was smuggled into the baggage car of a Galveston-bound train. Here he caught a boat and went to New York, eventually going to Canada and to Washington.

Wherever Jim Courtright went he kept in touch with friends in Fort Worth, and he longed to return. Finally he could stand it no longer. He returned to New Mexico and gave himself up. Months had passed and the charges against him were all but forgotten. He was cleared and returned to his family in Fort Worth.

During Courtright's absence, Luke Short had set himself up as king of the Fort Worth gamblers. He had been chased out of Dodge City and he had fought and gambled his way through the toughest days in Tombstone. His nerve could match any man's. As prince of the gamblers, Short had introduced keno to Fort Worth, which many citizens considered to be a fleecing game. Courtright was hired to clean it up and in doing so he made an enemy of Luke Short. Something had to happen when two such men were out to get each other.

It happened on the night of February 8, 1887. As there was only one witness to the act, the facts are vague, but it appears that Courtright and Short met on the street. There were some words and Courtright accused Short of going for his gun. At the same time Courtright made a motion toward his own gun. Short beat him to the draw and the first shot dropped big Jim. Then Short pumped four bullets into him.

The funeral was one of the largest in Fort Worth with fire bells tolling and all business at a standstill. Long Hair Jim Courtright was never beat to the draw but once. That mistake cost him his life.

BEN THOMPSON

8.

BEN THOMPSON

THE TWO-GUN MARSHAL OF AUSTIN

BEFORE BEN THOMPSON became marshal of San Antonio, Texas, he was a killer with a price on his head. He and his brother Billy—it was hard to tell which was the more desperate character—were both dead shots without the slightest regard for human life. They had bullied their way through cow town after cow town, terrorizing the country wherever they went.

Like most of the bad men of his day, Ben Thompson revealed little of his early life, and even the place of his birth is in dispute—some say it was Texas; others claim it was England or Nova Scotia. The year was about 1843.

Ben's boyhood days appear to have been spent in Austin, Texas, where he followed the printer's trade. He was tall and erect and even as a lad he liked fine clothes.

Following one printer's job after another, Ben finally found himself in New Orleans where he fought a duel and killed his opponent. Friends helped him escape, but he had taken his first human life and after that it seemed commonplace.

When the Civil War broke out Ben joined the Confederate Army and became the bad man of his regiment, ending by killing a sergeant. After the war he was arrested for killing a man, but

49

escaped to Mexico where he served with the forces of Maximilian. Upon his return to Texas he was again arrested and served two years in prison for assault to kill. In 1870 Ben stepped out of prison and headed for the gambling halls of the western cow towns.

He arrived in Abilene, Kansas, during its heyday. After winning a sizable sum of money in a card game, Ben teamed up with another gambler and gunman, Phil Coe, and opened the famous Bull's Head Saloon.

Wild Bill Hickok, who was then marshal of Abilene, accused Coe of cheating the cowboys at cards. Coe immediately threatened to kill Wild Bill. Trouble came a few weeks later when Coe was celebrating wildly with a group of Texans. Hickok tried to stop the Texans from shooting up the town and Phil Coe challenged him. They were standing only a few feet apart and opened fire simultaneously. Hickok fatally wounded Coe, and Ben Thompson never forgave the marshal.

Shortly after the shooting of his partner, Ben Thompson went to Ellsworth, Kansas, another cow town famed for its street fights and tough characters. A few days later his brother Billy arrived and Ellsworth was in for a wild ride. Here Ben set up gambling tables in Joe Brennan's place and he and Billy ruled Ellsworth to suit themselves.

The end of the Thompsons' reign of terror in Ellsworth came with the shooting of Sheriff Whitney by Billy Thompson after a general street brawl. Both Ben and Billy were eventually acquitted, but Ellsworth was no longer a healthy place for them to practice their gambling trade.

A noted gunman by this time, Ben hired out to the Atchison, Topeka and Santa Fe Railroad during its fight with the Denver and Rio Grande Railroad over the Royal Gorge site. Ben's job was to hold off the Denver and Rio Grande workers until the Santa Fe could lay its tracks. When he suddenly left the job, it was claimed that the Denver and Rio Grande people bought him off.

Ben now returned to his gambling profession in Austin where he was very popular with the cattlemen, and soon he was part owner of a popular gambling spot. His interest in the place, however, did not prevent him from shooting it up one night. Customers rushed through the doors and dived out windows as Ben blasted the place with both guns.

With many friends among the sporting element, Ben ran for city marshal, but was defeated. Determined to have the job, he ran a second time and won. By this time he was complete boss of Austin's killers—the type of man who would frequently dress up in high hat and

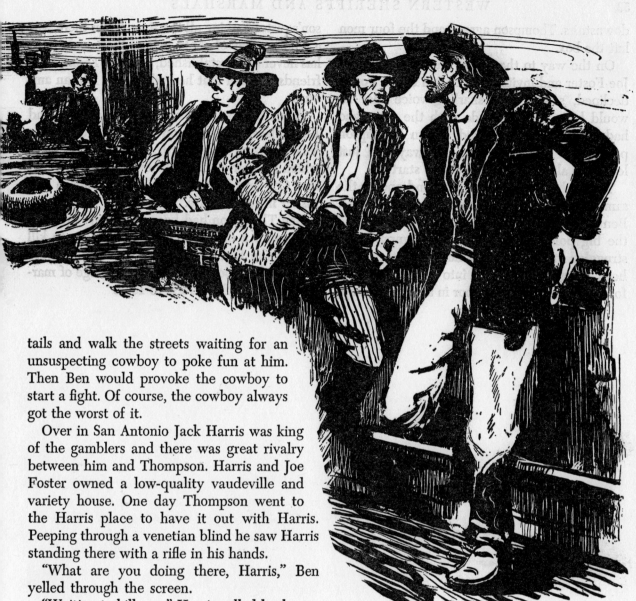

tails and walk the streets waiting for an unsuspecting cowboy to poke fun at him. Then Ben would provoke the cowboy to start a fight. Of course, the cowboy always got the worst of it.

Over in San Antonio Jack Harris was king of the gamblers and there was great rivalry between him and Thompson. Harris and Joe Foster owned a low-quality vaudeville and variety house. One day Thompson went to the Harris place to have it out with Harris. Peeping through a venetian blind he saw Harris standing there with a rifle in his hands.

"What are you doing there, Harris," Ben yelled through the screen.

"Waiting to kill you," Harris called back.

Thompson jerked out his pistol and fired three times so fast it sounded like a single shot. Harris fell with a hole in his forehead before he could lift his rifle to fire. Ben was acquitted of the killing under the old Texas law that said two armed men could fight it out as long as one wasn't shot in the back.

The killing of Jack Harris was not forgotten by the gamblers of San Antonio and especially by Harris' old partner, Joe Foster. Twenty months later, in 1884, Ben was invited to visit San Antonio and attend a good old-time jamboree at the old Harris vaudeville house. Suspicious, Ben took an old friend with him, King

Fisher, deputy sheriff of Uvalde County and also a man handy with a gun.

After pausing at the bar for a drink, Thompson and Fisher went upstairs to a box to watch the special show. There they were joined by Billy Sims, now co-owner of the house with Joe Foster, and by a big Mexican policeman named Coy.

Bored with the show, Ben Thompson insisted upon talking about his killing of Jack Harris in this very theater. King Fisher said he had come to the theater to be amused, not to discuss the killing of Jack Harris. When Thompson persisted, Fisher suggested they retire to the bar downstairs. Thompson agreed and the four men left the box.

On the way to the stairs, Thompson spotted Joe Foster and invited him to join them. Foster declined, saying in a snarling voice that he would have nothing to do with the man who had killed his good friend. When Thompson persisted, Foster said, "Go on away and just leave me alone." Then the action started.

Taking his gloves in his left hand and at the same time drawing his pistol with his right, Ben slapped Foster in the face. At this second the big policeman grabbed at Thompson and struggled for the gun. A bullet whizzed past his head. King Fisher jumped into the fight and the four men crashed to the floor in a heap, Thompson's pistol barking all the time. Then there was a whole volley of shots—where they came from has never been established, but Ben Thompson's friends claimed that he had walked into an ambush.

When the smoke cleared, Ben Thompson and King Fisher lay dead on the floor. Joe Foster was crawling away with a big wound from which he later died. At the inquest it was found that Coy and Foster had killed Thompson and Fisher in self-defense.

Ben Thompson had been living on borrowed time, with a dozen or more men eager to kill him at the first chance. He was a killer pure and simple although he wore the badge of marshal in Austin from 1882 to 1884.

JACK HELMS

JACK HELMS

9.

JACK HELMS

THE SHERIFF WHO MET THE TEXAS KILLER

A BRAVE but foolhardy sheriff was Jack Helms of Texas. Of his bravery there was certainly never any question. He proved that time and time again in the battle for existence in rough and ready DeWitt County in southern Texas. He could handle a gun as good as the next man, and he was handy with a knife. His weakness was that he was needlessly reckless in the face of a man like John Wesley Hardin, one of the Southwest's most ruthless killers, and that he allowed himself to be drawn into taking sides in a local feud.

The Taylor-Sutton feud flared up over the kind of incident that was overlooked many times in the early days of the West. Once such a feud started, however, only death could end it for, with everybody in the county involved, it was bound to continue until one side or the other was completely wiped out.

Charlie Taylor, an ex-Confederate soldier, was arrested and charged with stealing cattle. He claimed that he hadn't been stealing at all, but was only taking unbranded mavericks, as was the custom for many years. He failed to convince the authorities, but his conviction of his own innocence was such that he bolted jail and took to the hills.

A posse of deputy sheriffs, headed by William Sutton and including Jack Helms, took after Charlie. Overtaking the fleeing man, Sutton shouted at him to halt, but Charlie kept right on going as fast as his winded bronc could run. Sutton threw down on him and shot Charlie from his horse. He died a few days later.

The Taylors were fighting people and not the kind to stand by and see one of their kin slain, no matter what the charge. A young cousin of the dead man, Buck Taylor, stormed into Clinton with the avowed purpose of settling the score with William Sutton, who was himself hardly out of his 'teens and a handsome lad with a reckless abandon for his own safety.

The two gun slingers met in a saloon. Words flew back and forth. "I'll see you later," Buck warned.

"I'm ready right now," Sutton flaunted.

That was enough for Buck, and the two men went for their guns. Shots roared through the room. When the smoke cleared, Sutton, although wounded, stood over the dead Buck, a forty-four in each hand, and threatened the Taylor sympathizers.

"Clear out!" yelled Sutton. "Or I'll blast every last one of you!"

From then on it was war. How many men were killed will never be known, but a reign of terror swept over several counties, and neutral people were in danger of their lives because both factions viewed any fence-sitter with suspicion.

Because of this explosive situation a vigilante committee was formed in DeWitt County, headed by another William Sutton, known as Billy. Allied with the Sutton faction was the DeWitt County sheriff, Jack Helms.

At the head of the Taylor clan was old Creed Taylor, a veteran of many fights with Indians and Mexicans. Allied with him was the most heartless killer in Texas, John Wesley Hardin, an in-law of the clan.

Jack Helms cut a fine figure in the black suit he always wore, with his wide-brimmed hat and fancy spurred boots. Thick-chested and heavily bearded, Helms was no man to tangle with as he rode the county in the name of the law. About the only thing anyone had against him was the fact that he allowed himself to support one side against the other in the deadly Taylor-Sutton feud.

Helms's chief deputy, John B. Morgan, was a blustery man, who inclined to heavy drinking. He was no credit to his badge and aroused the anger of a number of people who would normally have backed the sheriff. Wes Hardin in particular hated Morgan, and it was well known in DeWitt County that each man was out to get the other.

The private feud between Hardin and Helms's chief deputy came to a head in a Cuero saloon in April 1873. Hardin was standing at the bar chatting and drinking when Morgan strutted in.

"I'm going to arrest you," the deputy said.

Hardin looked at the man coldly, finished his drink, turned on his heels, and walked out into the dirt street. Morgan followed him, made a

move for his pistol, and demanded his surrender. Hardin's hand flashed to his gun, came up with it, and fired from the hip. Morgan spun crazily and dropped with a bullet through his forehead. He was not the first, nor the last man to make the fatal mistake of drawing on John Wesley Hardin.

A month or so after the slaying of Morgan, Jack Helms and Hardin met in the neutral territory of Wilson County, supposedly to discuss some sort of a truce between the Taylors and the Suttons.

The meeting place was a small village. Both sides brought along a small army of men, and the local citizens, certain that something was going to happen, made themselves scarce. While the two roughly dressed armies sized each other up in the spring sun, Helms and Hardin met in the back room of a shack saloon, each flanked by two gun-laden henchmen.

Hardin spoke first and got right to the point. "You haven't come here to make peace, Helms. You intend to ambush us when we leave!"

As quick as a flash, he had his pistols out and,

covering Helms and his boys, he backed from the room and gave his men orders to ride.

That was the end of the truce meeting. Whether or not Jack Helms had really intended to trick Hardin and his men will never be known, but Hardin must be given credit for anticipating such a move and for backing out without touching off a pitched battle. Hardin immediately spread word among the Taylor faction to shoot the Helms men on sight. It was now war to the finish and no quarter given.

In the weeks that followed, fights flamed up wherever a Taylor met a Sutton. A Taylor man was killed in front of his store in Thomaston. Merchants closed their stores and townspeople remained behind locked doors, fearful that the battle would start at any second of night or day. Night riders scoured the country in search of each other and, wherever they met, there was killing on both sides.

Jim Taylor, one of Creed's sons, assumed command of the Taylor clan by outliving several slain leaders. One day he walked into a saloon to find himself surrounded by Helms men. Nowhere could he locate a friendly face. It was too late to turn back, and once he turned on that crowd someone was bound to let go with a blast. He walked straight to the bar and ordered a drink.

Word was carried to Jack Helms, who was playing cards in a back room. The sheriff sauntered in, walked quietly up to Taylor, drew his pistol, and shoved it into Taylor's back.

"You're under arrest, Taylor," he said. "Come on now, get going!"

"For what?" asked Taylor, lifting his hands.

"Because I want to arrest you!" snapped the sheriff.

"Don't move one inch, Helms!" came a voice from the doorway. "Or you'll be dead!"

There at the door stood Hardin, legs spread apart, his big sombrero tilted at a reckless angle. His two six-shooters covered the crowd and backed up his words.

Sheriff Helms looked at him, hardly believing his eyes, still holding his own gun in Jim Taylor's back.

"Put your pistol on the bar," commanded Hardin.

Helms hesitated, sizing up the situation, and then decided to try to beat Hardin at shooting—Hardin, the master gunman! For just one fraction of a second, Helms's Colt turned in the direction of Wes Hardin. Still keeping the crowd covered, Hardin fired twice with the gun in his left hand. The sheriff's pistol clanked to the floor. For a moment, Helms reeled crazily, spinning on his high-heeled boots, then he careened over on his back.

Even before Jack Helms hit the floor, Hardin's guns blazed again and three more bullets hit the dying sheriff as he went down.

The crowd stood with frozen faces as Hardin and Taylor backed out of the saloon. On the floor lay a dead sheriff—and a reckless one, who was in the end no match for his opponent.

JEFF MILTON

10.

JEFF MILTON

THE SOUTHERN GENTLEMAN WHO TAMED THE TEXAS KILLER

ONE OF THE TOUGHEST BORDER TOWNS of the Southwest was El Paso. For years multiple-notched gunmen had had things more or less their own way there, and peace officers came and went with great regularity—while the gamblers, the killers, and the toughs stayed on.

In 1894 El Paso got a new chief of police—Jeff Milton, one of the West's bravest law officers. At the same time El Paso was the headquarters of the ruthless gunman who slew Jack Helms—John Wesley Hardin.

From the time he was a callow youth Hardin's life had been one long trail of reckless killings. When he was twenty-one he could, and

did, boast of thirty-nine men dead from his fast and blazing guns. Wherever he went he was feared, and no man dared challenge him—until Jeff Milton came along.

Milton and Hardin first met in a saloon. As usual, the killer was wearing his two guns, which was against the law. The new chief of police intended to enforce that law.

"Take off those guns and check them at the bar," Jeff ordered.

Hardin looked Jeff over with his cold gray eyes. In calm and calculated words, he said, "Do you know who you're talking to?"

"Obviously I do," replied Milton, "and I'm

not at all impressed. You may have more notches on your guns than anybody in Texas, but as long as I'm chief of police here, you are no better than anybody else, and I intend to treat you like all law breakers. Now hand over those guns before trouble starts!"

It was one of Jeff's longest speeches on record. By the time he was through, the bar had emptied in anticipation of the gun battle about to start. Hardin had a powerful compulsion to kill Jeff on the spot, but something told him that here was a man with the deadly intention of backing up his words. Hardin stalled for the precise second to get the drop on Milton.

"I take off my guns for no man!" sneered the killer, maneuvering for a favorable position.

"Then I am going to kill you in just five seconds unless you drop your gun belt."

Three seconds ticked off, then four. Jeff made the slightest movement towards his gun. It was enough for the killer.

"Don't shoot," Hardin said, unbuckling his gun belt. "You win, chief. I'll abide by the law."

"That's all I ask," Milton stated calmly. "I have every right to kill you—and possibly I should rid the world of you, but as long as you know I mean business, and you respect our laws in El Paso, I will leave you alone, but make one bad move, Hardin, and I will kill you without further warning."

The man who so coolly faced this hardened killer had one of the most unusual backgrounds

of any of the peace officers of the West. Jeff Davis Milton grew up on the beautiful plantation of Sylvania in Florida, where his father was the governor, but his gracious home life never appealed to him. He dreamed of following the road of excitement and adventure to the great frontiers of the West.

Fishing and hunting were his favorite pastimes and he became an expert shot. At fifteen he quit school to take a clerk's job in a store—a far cry from his dream of chasing Indians, hunting buffalo, and fighting outlaws. Only a year later, however, he was on his way to Texas to live with an uncle, a good horse under him and a Winchester forty-four strapped to his saddle.

Punching cows and herding horses were more to Jeff's liking, but after a taste of the West, he had his eyes set on the Texas Rangers, that famous outfit of outlaw tamers known wherever gunfighters gathered. Jeff was only eighteen but, being a husky lad with a thin, scraggly mustache, he was able to pass as twenty-one. In July 1880, he was sworn in and headed on his way to the Ranger station at Hackberry Springs. Here he was trained to handle a gun by some of the West's most famous gunslingers, to ride, and to handle himself in any situation.

From Hackberry Springs, Jeff was soon riding with his company on scouting trips across the wide plateaus and into the rip-roaring cow towns of the Stoked Plains. Two railroads were building west through the country, and the towns that mushroomed at the end of the rails were tough and dangerous. It was one of Lance Corporal Jeff's duties to keep order in these towns.

When the railroads were completed and the new towns had settled down, the Rangers turned to other things. They were Indian scouts and they assisted ranchers searching for ranges. They escorted travelers across the hot and thirsty land, guarded surveying parties, and dogged the ever-present outlaws and bad men.

Jeff Milton stayed with the Rangers three years and, when he left them, he knew the rugged land north of the Rio Grande like the back of his hand.

Sheriff Charlie Nevill, of Val Verde County in Texas, aware of Jeff's record in the Rangers, summoned him to be his deputy. The boy from Florida mounted his horse and was off on the trail of bold and desperate men. Nevill was the first of many sheriffs Jeff Milton was to serve.

Some men can stay put, but Jeff Milton had to be constantly on the move in search of new places and new adventures. After working

a gun, of his knowledge of plains and mountains, of his ability to rough it with the toughest men of the West. To make his job as deputy sheriff at Socorro more interesting, he became at the same time a detective for the Central New Mexico Stock Association. When he was not on the trail of a desperado for the sheriff,

on the enormous I.C.C. Ranch as a cowhand, he drifted into western New Mexico and was grabbed up by Sheriff Bill Russell to be his deputy at Socorro. Here Jeff settled down long enough to round up the notorious Johnson gang of rustlers operating in the Black Range country.

Jeff Milton could kill a bad man as quick as any peace officer, but he preferred to negotiate rather than kill. Indeed, there was something about Jeff that appealed to the sense of pride and fair play in many brave but desperate characters. But Jeff could kill—and did—when necessary.

For a man of Milton's background, a life among cowboys and outlaws was a strange choice, but to Jeff nothing could have been more interesting. He was proud of his skill with

he was running down rustlers for the cowmen.

No place could hold Jeff Milton very long. He was soon on the trail again, rounding up cattle in San Marcial County, spending a week or so as deputy to Sheriff Commodore Perry Owens in Arizona, and then riding the Arizona-Mexico border as a patrolman for the U.S. Customs Service. It was the kind of a challenge Jeff Milton specialized in. He was to ride alone along the border from Nogales to the Gulf of California—a burning, waterless inferno—in search of smugglers.

In 1889 the border patrol became a victim of politics and the entire force was let go. Jeff's idea of a rest was to go prospecting and hunting in the Patagonia Mountains south of Tucson. He had barely killed his first deer when word came from Sheriff Fasion Shaw of Pinal County, who wanted Jeff as his deputy. Jeff could not resist the urge to be in the saddle again.

Up to this point, most of Jeff Milton's years of service on the side of the law had brought him very low pay, and although he had captured many wanted men, it seemed that someone else usually got the reward. In 1890, considering his financial condition for the first time in his life, Jeff turned to horse trading. When this did not pay off, he got a job firing a locomotive running out of El Paso.

In everything Jeff Milton undertook he was a perfectionist. It was no different with his railroad job. Soon the new fireman was promoted to conductor, and then the Pullman Company offered Jeff the run from El Paso to Mexico City. Jeff accepted, but in a few months he had tired of the job and was eager to take on the more active duties of a peace officer.

It was then he was offered the difficult job of chief of police of the lawless town of El Paso. In El Paso he had to deal not only with the notorious Hardin but also with an equally feared outlaw, John Selman, who killed in cold blood merely to place another notch on his gun. When Selman drifted into El Paso he had twenty dead men to his credit.

The man who had faced Hardin and come away alive managed to tame Selman in much the same manner, but in the end Hardin and Selman pretty effectively managed to wipe each other out. A few months after Selman had had some of the bite taken out of him by chief of police Milton, he walked into the Acme Saloon and saw Hardin sitting in a card game. Selman unceremoniously drew his forty-five and let Hardin have it in the back of the head. The case against Selman for killing Hardin was still in the courts when George

Scarborough, as the papers said, "transferred the case to a higher court" by killing the killer of John Wesley Hardin.

When the gamblers of El Paso attempted to bribe Jeff Milton, he turned in his badge and went to work for Wells, Fargo & Company as an express agent and guard combined. He spent a lot of time riding in express cars and in the saddle, hunting down highwaymen and outlaws of all descriptions. At the same time, he served as a deputy U.S. marshal and as a special Ranger for the State of Texas.

On one occasion Wells, Fargo had a shipment of several million dollars in gold going to California. Jeff was asked to hire a number of guards to see the shipment through. He declined to take the responsibility for the job if he had to hire additional guards, but he offered to guard the gold shipment himself.

"I know what I can do," he told Wells, Fargo. "I don't know what other men can do." He rode the shipment alone and nobody bothered it.

Surviving innumerable battles with outlaws, singly and in gangs, Jeff continued to roam from one job to another wherever the opportunity for excitement was greatest. In 1904 he joined the Immigration Service as a border agent. His duty consisted of breaking up the gangs smuggling Chinese workers into the United States.

He spent his last years in the desert country of southern Arizona, where he died in 1947 at eighty-five years of age. He had met the worst men in the whole wide West, and not one of them had bested him. All his life Jeff Davis Milton had followed the call of high adventure, guided by the sense of honor that made him one of the West's outstanding officers of the law.

TOM SMITH OF FORT BEND

11.

TOM SMITH OF FORT BEND

WHEN THE BIG cattle kings of Wyoming decided upon a showdown war with the little ranchers and homesteaders who were rapidly fencing the ranges and preventing the free movement of their cattle across the open grasslands, they naturally needed a group of hard-shooting men who could enforce their will. For help they turned to Tom Smith, a roving Texas peace officer who was acquainted with every gunman of note in the state and was friendly with most of them.

Tom Smith was rooted in the wildness of the West from his birth, for he was born and grew up in Texas. Like most boys of the time, he spurned a formal education, preferring the more practical and exciting life of a cowboy. He learned to hunt, fish, ride, and shoot, and the rugged outdoor life molded him into a young man who could stand up to anyone. While still in his 'teens, he joined the great trail drives and tasted the clouds of dust kicked up by the bawling herds of longhorns plodding their way to the railheads in Kansas and Nebraska.

This was a school to Tom Smith's liking—fording swollen streams, fighting off marauding Indians, thrilling to the angry roar of a night stampede, eating, riding, and sleeping out in the open with real men.

The Texas of Tom Smith's youth was teeming with outlaw bands, and hundreds of men who were wanted for crimes in other states had flocked into the area where there was no law and the six-shooter settled all arguments. Private feuds were handled as individual affairs without benefit of courts as long as a man followed the law of the frontier, which was simple: don't shoot a disarmed man; don't shoot a man from the back. Presumably, if a man was armed and was shot from the front, he had a chance to defend himself and, if he failed to do so, that was his hard luck. To shoot a man in the back was murder; to face him and kill him was merely a "killing."

Under such conditions, it was the strong who survived the longest; the weak died young or moved to other parts. Tom Smith was no weakling. His prowess with a pistol made him a man to be respected. Soon he was serving as town marshal of one tough town after another, and he wore the badge of office with pride and dignity. He was game to tackle anything and, when the town of Taylor called him to clean up a gang of outlaws who frequented the Sanderson Saloon, Tom Smith polished up his Colts and accepted the challenge.

Sanderson was a surly, hot-headed bully with several notches on his gun, and he had successfully resisted all efforts of the law to close his place of business. When Smith arrived in Taylor, he strolled into Sanderson's place and confronted the bad man.

"I'll have no trouble here, Sanderson," the marshal stated. "You can operate as long as you behave yourself and force your customers to behave, but I'll close you up if you don't."

Sanderson roared his challenge. "Get out of here, and stay out. If you come back, it will be at your own risk, and I'll kick you out!"

The new marshal eyed the hard faces staring at him. Every one of those men was on Sanderson's side, and ready to shoot in an instant if Sanderson signaled.

"I will be back," declared the marshal, turning his back on Sanderson and slowly walking out.

A few days later, the marshal was polishing his high black boots when word came that a cowboy had been robbed at Sanderson's place. Smith finished his boots, put them on, and headed alone down the street to the saloon. As he walked through the swinging doors, Sanderson grabbed his gun, but he was a split second too late. Standing over the dead gunman's sprawled form, the marshal announced, "This saloon is closed for good. My advice to you guys is to get out of town before sundown if you want to live."

Before the sun set that night, Taylor was a very quiet little cow town, and the Sanderson gang was broken up.

Later on, Tom Smith became deputy sheriff of Williamson County, with headquarters at Georgetown. Having helped bring law and order to that community, Smith was determined

to preserve it. His idea of preventing trouble was to head it off before it arrived. About this time, Ben Thompson, himself a peace officer and a noted gunman, was riding high, wide, and handsome through Texas, recklessly causing disturbances wherever he went. Smith decided that there was no room for Thompson in Georgetown and sent the burly Texan this telegram: *"Your absence will be welcome in Georgetown. If you do decide to pay us a visit, however, suggest you bring a nice warm coffin. The ground gets very cold down here at night."* Thompson decided to do his hell-raising elsewhere.

Tom Smith was too active to remain very long in one place, and wherever there was gunfire, he somehow managed to be on the scene before it was over. A political feud was boiling up in the Fort Bend country on the Brazos River and real trouble was at hand. Tom Smith turned up as deputy sheriff in the troubled county.

The day after the elections was the moment of expected explosions. A large crowd was in town and excitement ran high as the two sides waited tensely for action. Smith and the sheriff watched the situation from the courthouse lawn, ready for any emergency, though it was folly to think that anyone could control the angry mobs.

From down the street came a pistol shot, and almost instantly guns roared from every side. A band of armed men rushed the courthouse to free the prisoners in the county jail. The sheriff and his deputy retreated to the courthouse steps and fought off the attack. A man joined them in defending their post. Almost instantly he was hit and toppled to the ground. Then the sheriff fell, riddled with bullets. Tom Smith fought on alone, emptying his own cartridge belt and then grabbing those of his dead friends. Dusk found the street thick with gun smoke, but Tom Smith was still at his position, firing at the flashes of gunfire across the street. By nightfall the mob dispersed and Tom Smith was in command after one of the most bitter fights in Texas history.

Tom Smith moved about Texas so frequently and served in so many counties that it is virtually impossible to keep track of him. He served faithfully those who employed him, and every cause became a crusade. He was an old hand at dealing with hardened criminals and he could be just as ruthless with anyone who opposed what he happened to be fighting for at the time.

And now the trouble spot was in Wyoming. Tom Smith answered the call to go to Cheyenne and discuss the problem with the officials of the Stock Association, which represented the largest and most powerful cattlemen in the state. Just who was right and who was wrong has never been settled, but Tom Smith went to work for the well-financed cattle barons in a war to exter-

minate the "rustlers," as the cattlemen seemed to have classified everyone who opposed them.

The Stock Association was rounding up a gang of paid gunmen from Utah and Colorado. They wanted Tom Smith to recruit another such gang from Texas. The pay was good—$2500 for Smith and $1000 per man, for the job and all expenses paid. These men were first to congregate secretly in Cheyenne, then go to Casper by special train, carrying enough equipment to outfit an army, and invade Johnson County, seat of the trouble, on horseback. A list of the "rustlers" to be exterminated was to be supplied the gunmen and a bounty of fifty dollars was to be paid for each one killed. It was an invasion, pure and simple, but it promised plenty of action, and that was for Tom Smith.

Knowing every gun-slinger from Arkansas to Arizona, Smith had no trouble in hiring his quota. They drifted into Cheyenne and awaited the big day. There each man was briefed in his specific duty of coldly and methodically running down "rustlers."

The invasion got off to an impressive start with almost militarylike precision, but in its first encounter with the enemy, things went wrong. Two so-called rustlers, Nick Rae and Nate Champion, were surrounded in their cabin at the KC Ranch and shot to death. This so infuriated the settlers of Johnson County that they formed an army of their own and besieged the hired invaders. Only the last-minute intervention of U.S. Army troops stationed at a near-by fort prevented the slaughter.

The gunmen and cattlemen participating in the invasion were rounded up and taken to Cheyenne under arrest, a new experience for Tom Smith who had himself arrested hundreds of men. The invaders were freed on bail after political repercussions that reached the White House, and the men separated pending the day of their trial.

At the hour the ex-invaders filed into the courtroom in Cheyenne, Tom Smith, who had played such an important role in the Johnson County War, was among the missing. On November 5, 1892, he had been killed in Oklahoma while arresting an outlaw—the kind of an exit everyone knew Tom Smith of Fort Bend was bound to make sooner or later.

JOHN SLAUGHTER

12.

JOHN SLAUGHTER

THE SHERIFF WHO DIDN'T BELIEVE IN JAILS

WHEN JOHN SLAUGHTER ACCEPTED the silvered sheriff's star of Cochise County, Arizona—one of the toughest, wildest, and most lawless sections of the United States—he had but one thing in mind, to make the place safe for the cattle business in which, more than anything else, he was interested.

Everyone who knew anything about John Slaughter fully expected him to make good his intention—or to die in trying. No one had any idea, however, that the tough little ex-Texan would accomplish the miracle in four short years—and almost singlehanded at that!

Slaughter didn't need the job of sheriff, although it paid a good deal of money, for he was a successful rancher and a man of considerable means, but he was stubbornly beset with the strange notion that a simple, law-abiding citizen had a right to pursue his own peaceful ways without interference from a gang of outlaws. He had seen the sheriffs of Cochise County—some good, some bad—come and go with disgusting regularity, while lawlessness increased every year. If no one else could clean up the mess, well, John Slaughter allowed that he could!

When Slaughter turned in his sheriff's star four years later, not only was he still alive, but Cochise County was as safe as any place in the United States. The outlaws and other assorted bad men he had encountered along the way were either under the ground or practicing their trades in other parts.

John Slaughter believed that a fearless law officer was the equal any time of the most blustering, trigger-happy bad man. The outlaws, he said, simply had to be made to understand that you meant business—a point he drilled home emphatically with the smoking end of his prized pearl-handled six-shooter.

Slaughter believed, too, that jail was no cure for a real outlaw. He contended that it merely cost the county good money to chase down and feed a scamp who would only laugh at you and start his depredations all over again when turned loose. His method was simpler: give a man a few hours to get out of the county. If he ignored your well-meant advice, kill him on sight!

When Sheriff Slaughter rode out to apprehend anyone stupid enough to hang around after being commanded to get going, he rode alone. When he met his man there were usually no useless words—only the lightning-swift drawing of two guns—and the sheriff's always barked first! There was no squirming, surly prisoner to lead back to town, no trial, no jail term. John Slaughter was the one-man law of Cochise County, and it was just about the most effective law any county ever had!

John Slaughter didn't look like a Western sheriff any more than he acted like one. A short man, he stood only about five feet six, even in his costly high-heeled and well-polished boots, but he was as tough and wiry as the cold blue steel of his six gun. He talked little, but every word he uttered was coldly measured and in deadly earnest.

He liked expensive, well-made clothes, but not the flashy outfits so dear to the professional gambler or roistering cowboy. His star was a badge of authority never abused. His pearl-handled forty-five, which he wore for fifty years without taking it off except for sleeping and eating—and then it was always within easy reach—was seldom drawn unless he intended to kill. Once he ordered a member of the notorious Curly Bill gang to leave Tombstone. The outlaw was standing at a bar with one drink under his belt and another on its way. He made an almost imperceptible move toward his gun. The steely glint in Slaughter's eyes spelled almost certain death. The customers in the drinking palace began scampering for cover. Without making the slightest motion toward his own gun, the sheriff spoke calmly. "I will count five," he said. "If I have to go for my gun I will kill you." Slowly he started counting. "One . . . two . . . three . . ."

The enraged outlaw looked John Slaughter squarely in the eyes, and it was then that he decided to live another day. Setting down his glass, he turned and walked toward the swinging doors. "And if I ever see you with as much as one foot in Cochise County," the sheriff called to him, "I will drop you dead in your tracks."

John Slaughter had a reputation in Arizona long before he moved to Cochise County. Born in Louisiana of parents who could trace their history back through all the wars to Colonial days, he was known as a fighter for his rights in a country where a man often had no rights other than those he could establish with a blazing gun.

In Texas, where the Slaughters settled when John was a small boy, he started handling a gun almost at the time he took his first steps alone. His father saw to that. He was a small boy and not very strong. On his father's ranch he was taught that if he expected to stay alive in the wild and lawless expanses of the Southwest, he would have to make up for his physical disadvantages by excelling with a six-shooter. "It makes up for the difference," his father used to tell him. John Slaughter developed an early skill with a pistol that few men could match and he determined that he would always hold his own against all odds and all kinds of people.

When the Civil War broke out, young Slaughter joined the Confederate Army, but he was ailing with tuberculosis and in less than a year he was discharged as unfit for military service. He returned to Texas, determined to grow strong through an active outdoor life. Somehow he managed to join up with the famous Texas Rangers, a body of hard-riding law enforcement officers noted for their rough-and-ready fighting tactics. It wasn't long before

Ranger Slaughter had won the respect of the toughest man in the outfit. Even in the Rangers he preferred to ride alone, depending upon his superior skill with a gun rather than on numbers. Here he developed the habits of vigilance that contributed so much to his surviving to the ripe old age of eighty-two.

Six years in the Rangers made a new man of John Slaughter—if still a small one. He quit and started ranching on his own in Texas, but he already had his eyes on the rich grasslands of the southeastern Arizona border country. In 1879, with a group of Texas cowboys, he drove a herd of cattle through the Indian-infested lands to Arizona and grazed them in an area east of Tombstone, which was then a wild and roaring mining camp. In the following year he started for Arizona again—this time for good—driving ahead of the wagons carrying his belongings, the three thousand remaining cattle comprising his herd. Accompanying him was a group of hand-picked Texas cowboys.

When Slaughter selected a cowhand, he was seldom wrong in his judgment of men. Young Billy Claiborne was one of the exceptions. Billy made the long and arduous drive with Slaughter from Texas to Arizona. He was impetuous and reckless and he wanted nothing better than to be known as a bad man. Slaughter tried to straighten him out before he got his fool head blowed off, but the kid wouldn't listen and that's exactly what happened to him.

It came very suddenlike for Billy. Frank, better known as "Buckskin," Leslie, a bartender at the Oriental Bar in Tombstone and a killer in his own right, was on duty when Billy came in offensively drunk. Fancying himself somewhat of a ladies' man, Buckskin objected to Billy's rough language in front of the dance floor girls. Billy told Frank to blow his horn in another direction. Leslie picked the kid up by the seat of his pants and forcefully escorted him out the swinging doors. Highly indignant at such treatment, Billy departed to find himself a shotgun, fully determined that Buckskin Frank would never throw anyone else out of a bar again.

Warned by a friend that Billy was waiting outside for him, Leslie removed his bartender's apron, carefully hung it up, and got out his forty-five. Laying his burning cigar on the polished bar, he slipped out a side door and sneaked along the adobe wall to the front of the saloon. Billy was standing there with his back to Leslie. "Billy," the bartender called calmly. The boy spun around and promptly fell dead with a bullet between the eyes. Buckskin Frank walked back into the bar, quietly put on his apron, and picked up the still-burning cigar. Turning to a customer, he said, "He died real nice!" Billy Claiborne was eighteen years old when they put him to bed with a shovel in Boot Hill. He wanted to be a bad man!

Slaughter's trail to Arizona was straight through the heart of dreaded Apache country, and the Apaches, as everyone knew, were the sworn enemies of all white men, the cruelest, craftiest, fightingest Indians of the whole Southwest. This mattered little to John Slaughter. His rights were his rights, Apaches, outlaws, or come what may. He met the Apache hordes head on and fought them to a standstill. They soon learned to respect the wiry little rancher from Texas.

When Slaughter arrived in Arizona with his second herd, he found that many of his cattle left in the San Bernardino Valley the year before had been driven off by rustlers. Looking around for his brand, he located a few head here and there mixed up with the cattle of other outfits. Naturally John Slaughter thought nothing of riding into these herds and cutting out his own cattle. Some of the cattlemen thought differently, however, and one angry rancher had the temerity to order Slaughter off his range. "Look here," John Slaughter said. "You know the rules here as well as I do. Any critter wearing my brand belongs to me and I aim to take it!"

After some sharp words, Slaughter ordered his men to cut out his cattle. "If you make a move to draw your gun," he warned, "I'll kill you!" He got his cattle and the Arizona ranchers learned that John Slaughter was a man of his word. By the time he reached Sulphur Springs Valley to the east of Tombstone, it was a well-established fact that the new rancher was a fearless fighter for his rights.

Tombstone, the roaring center and county seat of Cochise County where John Slaughter had selected to settle his family, was a rough-and-tumble mining community on the cactus- and brush-covered hills of the high desert and it was, as historians often reflected, "a town too tough to die!" As the immense riches of the mines around Tombstone became known, men of all professions flocked in by the thousands, most of them intent upon getting rich at the point of a gun or through their skill and trickery at the gambling tables.

The early vigilante committees who attempted to keep some semblance of law and order were booted out of the town as the gamblers and gun fighters moved in and took over. Two out of every three buildings in the gaudy, false-fronted business section became saloons or gambling dens, and the most notorious characters from the other hell-raising camps of the West swarmed to the new boom town en masse. The first cemetery grew so rapidly that it had to be enlarged at frequent intervals to accommodate those who died with their boots on. Speed on the draw determined the length of a man's stay above the ground as Tombstone became synonymous with everything wild, reckless, daring, and evil!

Some ten miles southwest of Tombstone was the town of Charleston on the banks of the San Pedro River where, because of the lack of water in Tombstone, the stamp mills for the mining district were located. If possible, Charleston was even wilder than Tombstone, although the point can be argued.

Across the rugged mountains and hot valleys to the east, in a small, well-watered canyon of the Chiricahua Mountains, nestled the little town of Galeyville—far from the sheriff's office and almost inaccessible from the Tombstone side. It was a resort, almost unmolested by the law, for a gang of outlaws and smugglers who posed as innocent and hard-working ranchers. Here Curly Bill Brocius, a bronzed, blue-eyed giant of a man with a flair for flashy clothes, made his headquarters and ruled the Galeyville outlaws.

On a ranch deep in the ravines and mountains adjoining the western side of Sulphur Springs Valley and not far from the town of Charleston, "Old Man" Clanton and his three sons had their headquarters. Along with a following of rustlers and bandits, the Clantons' main occupation consisted of running stolen Mexican cattle across the border for sale in Cochise County markets.

They had no rules, however, against stealing the cattle of their more law-abiding neighbors, of whom John Slaughter was now one.

Still a third gang of outlaws made their headquarters at the ranch of the McLowery brothers, Tom and Frank, across the valley from Old Man Clanton's hangout. The Clantons, the McLowerys, and Curly Bill's outfit could muster between them perhaps a hundred men and, located as they were strategically around the county, they combined forces to dominate the area.

This was the country into which John Slaughter moved his cattle and family and planned to settle down to raising beef for the Army. On all sides of him—in every canyon and around every water hole—lurked outlaws and rustlers, and the towns were crowded with bad men of every description, great and small. Anybody but John Slaughter would have kept right on going!

Slaughter's first brush with the Clantons came when he caught Ike Clanton on his range looking over a fine herd of cattle. Taking orders from a cattleman—and a little one at that—was a new experience for a Clanton, but when Slaughter told Ike to get off his range, the outlaw had better sense than to argue.

"And if I ever find you on my land again, or any of your gang, I'll kill you on the spot!" Slaughter warned the intruder. "I'm here to stay if I personally have to kill every rustler in Arizona!" That was language any Clanton could understand. Ike rode away and reported the incident to his father. "He'll let his guard down someday," said Old Man Clanton. "That'll be the end of John Slaughter!"

But John Slaughter's guard was never down. He had learned four rules to live by, and the fact that he outlived the scores of men who swore to kill him can be attributed to his careful observance of these rules. He never, never sat or stood in a position where his back could become a target—even in his own home or in his office. He never rode into a spot from which he could be ambushed, often riding miles out of his way to avoid a place where a gunman could be concealed. He never rode out in a buckboard without leading a saddled horse behind. He never removed his gun from his body except when it was absolutely necessary.

Once Slaughter set out on a cattle-buying trip, carrying considerable money on his person. His sharp eyes caught the figures of two men concealed at a curve in the trail ahead. He avoided the ambush, but upon his return home he learned that two of the Charleston outlaws, Ed Lyle and Cap Stillwell, had planned to rob him. Slaughter rode straight into Charleston and, walking up to Lyle, said, "Get out of this country, Lyle! Get out immediately!"

"But I'm not armed," protested Lyle. "You can't shoot an unarmed man!"

"You'd better get armed quick then," snapped Slaughter. "I'll be back tonight and if I find you here, I'll shoot to kill!"

Stillwell was in a saloon when Slaughter sauntered in. The outlaw went for his gun but found himself looking down the muzzle of Slaughter's silvered Colt before he could draw. "I have every right to kill you, Stillwell," Slaughter said. "I'm giving you until dark to get out of town!" Lyle and Stillwell were never seen in those parts again.

Aside from his constant clashes with the outlaws, Slaughter had to fight off the frequent

boy and again as a Texas Ranger. He knew the ways of the red men as well as they did themselves, and he and his cowboys retaliated with a ferocity that even the Apaches understood, frequently chasing the fleeing Indians far into Mexico. Before long the Apaches showed a great deal of respect for the cattle and horses wearing the Slaughter brand.

Inevitably John Slaughter became a man marked for death by many of his bitter enemies. One of these men was Doc Holliday, a frail eastern dentist who had come west for his health. In the wide-open town of Tombstone he had recovered remarkably and was known to one and all as a deadly, cold-blooded killer.

Slaughter suspected that Holliday had once tried to hold him up. Being a man of few words and direct action, the rancher told the ex-dentist never to make the mistake again unless he hankered to join the boys six feet under in Boot Hill back of town. These were pretty threatening words, and Doc had killed more than one man for less. He marked off a place on his gun for the notch John Slaughter would one day add.

But the days when Doc Holliday could bully his way around Tombstone were rapidly com-

A TOWN TOO TOUGH TO DIE

raids of Apaches crossing the border from Mexico. Their cattle was being stolen by the Charleston and Galeyville outlaws, and they saw no wrong in fighting back. Unfortunately for the poor Indians, John Slaughter was right in the middle. He had fought the Indians as a

ing to an end. He was a close friend of Wyatt Earp, a deputy U.S. marshal who enjoyed quite a reputation as a gunman himself. Earp, his brothers Morgan and Virgil, who were city marshal and deputy sheriff respectively, and Johnny Behan, who was Cochise County's sheriff, along with the magnificent gun work of Doc Holliday, represented the law in Tombstone. In spite of their official positions, however, there were many who suspected that the members of the Earp clan were little better than the outlaws they pretended to subdue. It can be said with certainty that, whatever their real status, they carried on many secret dealings with shady characters.

An open feud between the Earp faction and the Clantons and McLowerys developed when the outlaws accused Doc Holliday of killing Bud Philpot, a member of the Charleston outlaws, during the holdup of a stagecoach. The climax came in October 1881 with a furious gun battle at the O. K. Corral in Tombstone when Doc Holliday and Wyatt and Virgil Earp opened fire on Ike and Billy Clanton and Tom and Frank McLowery, not all of whom were armed, as they prepared to leave town after a drinking spree. Billy Clanton and the Mc-Lowery brothers were killed, but Ike managed to mount his panicked horse and escape. The Earps and Holliday were exonerated but the incident led to warfare from ambush and, after the killing of several men on both sides, the remaining Earps and Doc Holliday rode out of Tombstone never to return.

To John Slaughter the capitulation of the Earps meant simply that the outlaws had wiped out what little law and order Tombstone could lay claim to. He and his wife had moved into town by this time where he was a familiar, but quiet figure on the streets of the town "too tough to die." He had taken no part in the Clanton-Earp feud because his sole interest was in raising cattle. Law enforcement, as he saw it, was a job for the officers of the law.

About this time Slaughter heard that one of the great Spanish land grants along the border was for sale. The land consisted of more than 70,000 acres, partly in Cochise County, but extending into Sonora, Mexico. Without looking at it, he bought the land and soon extended his holdings to more than 100,000 acres.

Meanwhile, with the departure of the Earps, Tombstone and Cochise County were becoming more lawless than ever. Honest people dared not go out at night, and even an armed man was taking his life in his hands to walk the streets by day. Cattle and horses were stolen from the ranches faster than they could be replaced. Bandits roamed the roads and a man could be killed for less than a dollar. Something had to be done, and in desperation the solid citizens of the county turned to John Slaughter and elected him sheriff.

"I'm a cattleman," said Slaughter when he heard the news, "but if I expect to have any cattle left, someone's sure got to clean up the country. I'll take the job!"

People who expected spectacular action were disappointed at first. The new sheriff organized no large posses; he appointed only a handful of trusted deputies. When the county offered to build a better jail to hold the outlaws everyone thought Sheriff Slaughter would be bringing in, he smiled and made about the longest speech of his career.

"I don't expect to fill the jail," he said. "I see no advantage of going to the great expense of tracking down an outlaw, arresting him at the risk of your neck, and bringing him back to Tombstone with the possibility of a gang rescue en route. When I get through, the only outlaws remaining in Cochise County will be dead ones!"

Sheriff Slaughter's first official act was to order the crooked gamblers, saloon hangers-on, petty thieves, and other undesirable characters to leave the county at once. There was a general exodus. For several months after that Tombstone saw him only on rare occasions when he would ride in and out of town on his familiar gray horse. He carried his message straight to the outlaw hideouts: "Get out of the county by sundown and stay out! This is your only warning!" They started scattering in all directions!

Word came one day that a party of five train robbers were holed up in the Whetstone Mountains some twenty-five miles northwest of Tombstone. A large group of men offered to go with Slaughter to round them up. He took two, and these, as it turned out, he didn't need. Slaughter's gun killed one of the outlaws, mortally wounded the second, and wounded the third man twice. The remaining two had left before the arrival of the three-man posse.

When John Slaughter rode out to recover stolen horses he always went alone. Whether it was in a few days, or in a few weeks, when he returned he was leading the stolen animals, but never a prisoner. When he was asked why he never brought back a horsethief, he always replied, "He resisted. He won't commit the crime again!" How many outlaws he did away with in this manner will never be known. John Slaughter seldom, if ever, boasted of his exploits.

Some of Cochise's citizens resented Slaughter's assumption that he was judge and jury—and often executioner—but everyone understood that only by such hard, quick action could the county be cleaned up. The kind of smoking-gun language spoken by John Slaughter was much more to the point than legal phraseology—and tremendously persuasive.

At the end of the first term of John Slaughter's kind of law, Cochise County was well on its way to becoming for the first time in its history a place where a man could expect to live from morning to night. He was almost unamiously re-elected for a second term. Serving out his fourth year, he refused to be elected for a third term. He considered his job done. He was forty-nine years of age and he wanted nothing more than to retire to the peace and quiet of his border ranch. He had brought safety to the deserts, to the mountains, and to the city streets of Tombstone, Galeyville, and Charleston. No longer was a man's life measured by the seconds required to draw his gun. The outlaws and gunmen he had not disposed of had taken themselves elsewhere. Wherever bad men gathered, it was agreed that John Slaughter was the toughest sheriff who ever drew a six-shooter.

Now and then the peace and quiet was broken by the raids of a band of renegade Indians, escaped from their reservation. When this happened, John Slaughter would ride again. During the many calm months between such incidents, he never once relaxed his life-long practice of vigilance. The silver-plated, pearl-handled Colt six gun that had served him so well for over fifty years was strapped to his hip in his eighty-second year when he died peacefully on the ranch he loved on Valentine's Day 1922—the last of the great sheriffs who tamed the West.

WYATT EARP

13.

WYATT EARP

THE MARSHAL WHO NEVER WALKED AWAY
FROM A FIGHT

A BOISTEROUS BAD MAN stumbled into a barber-shop in El Paso and went down the line of chairs slapping each customer in turn. When he got to the last chair, the half-shaved customer looked the bad man squarely in the eyes and said, "All right, if you're ready to die, go ahead and slap me!"

The bad man fingered his gun, looked at the customer for one instant, and bolted for the door. The customer was Wyatt Earp.

Possibly no Western peace officer earned as controversial a reputation as that enjoyed by Wyatt Earp while deputy U.S. marshal at Tombstone, Arizona, during the turbulent days of the 1880's. No one questioned that he enforced the law as he saw it, but there were those who claimed that he maimed, killed, and imprisoned men for so much per head, taking ev-ery advantage open to him. According to others, he was honest, diligent, and efficient. Still others said Earp was a killer of the deadliest type.

One thing is certain, however. Wyatt Earp was strictly business and he never turned his back on a fight. He had a calculating mind and always figured the percentages, which possibly explains why he never suffered a wound and died in bed at eighty.

Wyatt Earp's parents journeyed westward from Virginia, stopping along the way to add another child to their rapidly growing family. Wyatt was born in Illinois and raised in Kansas. As a boy of fifteen he made the dangerous trip to the West Coast, much of it through Indian country, and before long, while still in his 'teens, he was a hardened plainsman, holding his own with the best of the buffalo hunters.

Although Wyatt Earp appeared on the scene in many Western frontier towns, it was in Tombstone that his reputation was made. He arrived there in 1879 with an appointment as deputy United States marshal, and was soon followed by his brothers, James, Virgil, Morgan, and Warren.

When Sheriff Fred White was killed in a gun battle on the streets of Tombstone, Wyatt Earp wanted to be made sheriff, but the job went to John H. Behan. Because the Sheriff of Cochise County was also county assessor and tax collector and was permitted to keep ten per cent of the taxes collected, the sheriff's job was worth about $40,000 a year to the man in office. When Wyatt lost the appointment it started an enmity between the Earp brothers and the sheriff's office that lasted throughout Wyatt's stay in Tombstone.

three sets of officers and there were many charges that one or the other set was in cahoots with rustlers and outlaws.

Strangely enough, the Earps managed to be represented on two of the law-enforcement groups—Wyatt as deputy U.S. marshal, Morgan as a deputy town marshal, and Virgil as town marshal. James and Warren Earp did not remain long around Tombstone but, under the leadership of Wyatt, the remaining three Earps soon formed a clan that operated in open opposition to the sheriff's office.

The rich Tombstone mines brought bad men from all parts of the West into the wild country surrounding Tombstone. There stage-robbers, outlaws, and cattle thieves found safe refuge. The outlaw element was formed into a sort of a clan under the leadership of the Clantons and McLowerys, who were followed by a group of lesser cowboys.

The Clantons and the McLowerys became unfriendly with the Earps when Doc Holliday, a quick-triggered member of the Earp clan, was

To complicate things further there were in Tombstone three sets of peace officers: the deputy U.S. marshal, who was supposed to step in only when a Federal law was being violated; the county sheriff; and the city marshal, whose authority did not extend beyond the city limits. There was a great deal of jealousy among the

accused of a stagecoach holdup and the killing of Bud Philpot, a cowboy and member of the Clanton-McLowery group. Holliday was cleared of the crime but it was evident that the bad blood between the two groups would one day break into open warfare. Tombstone was not going to be large enough to contain both factions.

The climax came on October 26, 1881, in the fight at the O. K. Corral. On the previous day Ike Clanton and Tom McLowery had arrived in Tombstone in a light wagon, leading a saddle horse. On the next day, Billy Clanton and Frank McLowery rode in from Charleston and met them.

On their first night in town together, Ike Clanton got into a quarrel with Doc Holliday and refused Doc's invitation to step into the street and fight it out. Morgan Earp further added to the feud by abusing Ike and daring him to fight. There was a strong feeling around the bars of Tombstone that this was to be the long-expected showdown and things would explode into action any minute.

On the morning of the 26th, Virgil and Morgan Earp met Ike Clanton on the street carrying a gun, which was against the law. Although Ike did not resist being disarmed, the Earps

town for their ranch. Sheriff John Behan, sensing that trouble was about to start, went to the corral to disarm the cowboys. Ike Clanton showed that he was not armed, as did Tom McLowery. Billy Clanton and Frank McLowery refused to give up their arms, saying that they were leaving town. They were, in fact, preparing to mount their horses when they saw four men walking toward them down the middle of the street.

The four men were Morgan, Virgil, and Wyatt Earp and Doc Holliday. One man was heard to say, "If they want a fight, let them have it." Each of the Earps was wearing side arms. Doc Holliday carried his favorite weapon, a sawed-off shotgun, half concealed beneath his long coat.

Failing to disarm the cowboys, Sheriff Behan raced toward the approaching law officers and

knocked him to the ground. Later in the morning Wyatt met Tom McLowery and, although the latter was unarmed, Earp gave the cowboy a pistol whipping.

Early that afternoon the Clanton and McLowery brothers were at the O. K. Corral, where their horses were kept, preparing to leave

tried to persuade them to turn back, saying that the cowboys were leaving town. He was brushed aside, as the four men walked determinedly toward the corral.

As they neared the corral, Tom and Billy were leading their horses and were about to mount. The rifles on their saddles were in plain sight. Ike and Frank were standing near by.

"You have been looking for a fight," said Wyatt Earp. "You can have it."

Someone fired and the battle was on. Doc Holliday raised the shotgun to his hip and instantly killed Tom McLowery. Morgan Earp shot Billy Clanton and Wyatt dropped Frank McLowery, who staggered into the street trying to pull his pistol. Ike bolted and ran. Virgil Earp was wounded in the leg.

Altogether some twenty-five or thirty shots were fired in the O. K. Corral fight. Three men were dead, but the people of Tombstone knew that this was far from the end of the feud between the Earps and the outlaw rustlers. While the Earps and Holliday were arrested for the killings, they were exonerated on the grounds of "having acted as peace officers in performance of their duties."

From the moment the McLowerys and Billy Clanton were killed, the Earp clan—from five to eight men—usually appeared in public together and always heavily armed. They expected trouble. On a stormy night in early 1882, only a few months later, someone fired a shotgun slug into Virgil Earp. He was badly injured and laid up for a long time.

Some two months later Morgan Earp let down his guard while playing a game of pool and paid for this carelessness with his life. Someone fired through a back door and dropped Morgan dead in his tracks as he lifted his cue.

On the next day Virgil, still slowly recovering from his gunshot wounds, and Wyatt started for California by train with their brother's body. An attempt was made to kill other members of the Earp party as it boarded the train, and Wyatt Earp killed Frank Stilwell, whom he suspected of having fired the shot that took Morgan's life.

It was clear to Wyatt Earp that life in Tombstone was going to continue to be one shooting after another until one of the two factions was wiped out. He made the decision to leave, and as far as is known no Earp ever returned to Arizona.

After leaving Tombstone, Wyatt went to Colorado where the Governor refused to extradite him for the charge of killing Frank Stilwell. After that Wyatt seemed content to seek out boom towns, eventually going to the Yukon and to Alaska in search of the life he liked. Entering the real estate business, he became a wealthy man and died in Los Angeles in 1929 at eighty-one years of age.

Warren, the youngest Earp, was killed by a rustler in New Mexico. Virgil died a natural death in Goldfield, Nevada.

There are those who still remember the familiar figure of Wyatt Earp in Tombstone—his gaunt eyes, his long face and square jaw, the loose-limbed powerful frame, and the distinctive dress that made him stand out in any crowd. He was better than six feet tall and wore a black broad-brimmed hat, a black frock coat, black trousers tucked into fancy boots, white shirt, and black string tie. He could pass for a gambler, a gunman, or a law officer.

COMMODORE PERRY OWENS

14.

COMMODORE PERRY OWENS

THE SHERIFF WHO RODE ALONE

HOLBROOK, ARIZONA, was looking forward to meeting the new sheriff of Apache County. In fact, the new sheriff had been in office only a week, and word was already going around that he was too smart—or too cowardly, as some people put it—to interfere in the lawlessness of this tough little cow town with its reputation for making short work of sheriffs.

Holbrook was near the headquarters ranch of the Aztec Land and Cattle Company, called the Hash Knife outfit after the shape of its brand. The Hash Knife cowboys were in the habit of riding into Holbrook with guns blazing, shooting out the lights at dances, and otherwise making the town one of the wildest in the wild Western tradition. Several Hash Knife men were also known killers and they roamed around Holbrook without fear of the law.

Holbrook was also the center of the notorious Tewksbury-Graham feud which raged in Pleasant Valley and blazed up wherever members of the two factions met.

On one side were the Grahams, who had come from Iowa. The most ruthless killers in their faction were the five Blevins brothers along with their half-brother, Andy Cooper. Since he was wanted for killing a man in Texas, he had found it convenient to take a different name. Andy was considered the best gunman on either side of the feud. A rough, boastful fellow, he was fantastically quick on the draw and an experienced rustler and horse thief. He terrorized the Holbrook section and for ten years had defied the law to lay a hand on him.

On the other side was John Tewksbury, who had come to Arizona from Boston, with his three half-breed sons, who were all expert marksmen.

The Tewksburys and the Grahams had quarreled over stolen cattle and sheep for many years. The struggle broke into open warfare, and both sides swore to fight it out until not a member of the other group remained alive. Every man who remained in the valley was drawn into the conflict, in which no quarter was asked or given. An enemy was hunted like a wild animal and death was the penalty for an unguarded moment. All attempts by law officers to end the fight were futile.

This was the explosive situation in Holbrook as the new sheriff—Commodore Perry Owens—rode across the hot desert floor with a warrant in his pocket for the arrest of Andy Cooper on a charge of horse stealing.

The new sheriff's name was a joke to the cowboys. It was no joke to the sheriff, however. Back in Tennessee his mother had named him for the great hero of the Battle of Lake Erie. When Commodore was in his 'teens, he headed west with a wagon train and went to Texas where he somehow managed to get a good education before becoming one of the trail drivers of the vast herds of longhorns moving into Kansas.

By the time Owens left Texas he had earned a reputation as a man quick on the draw with his black-butted forty-fours. He wore his guns butt forward on each hip, a style that evoked a lot of laughs from men who did not know how handy Commodore was with his artillery.

Owens was also renowned in Texas for his fearless defense of a wagon train against a band of attacking Indians. He fought them off almost singlehanded and was asking for more when the foolish Indians decided to call it off.

When the civic leaders of Apache County heard of the invincible Owens, they invited him to run for sheriff. Bored with trail driving and guarding wagon trains, Owens accepted and won the race easily. One of his first official acts was to call on the county clerk to find out what warrants were outstanding.

"Here's one," said the clerk. "It's for a fellow named Andy Cooper over in Holbrook. It's been here a long time—no one had the stomach to serve it. Those who tried are dead."

"I'll serve it," said the new sheriff.

As Commodore Perry Owens rode along on his big bay, he looked like a man from another country. He preferred the outmoded dress of a plainsman—a wide-brimmed, flat-topped prairie hat and the fringed buckskin jacket of the buffalo hunter. His chaps were silver-studded leather instead of the rawhide type popular in the area. His hair was shoulder length and he was clean-shaven except for a small mustache. His eyes were steel blue and his face was a picture of kindness, but he could mean business—as he did on this particular mission.

Owens arrived in Holbrook in mid-afternoon. He walked his horse through the main street to the combination blacksmith shop and livery stable, where he asked a cowboy named Bill Gard if Andy Cooper was in town.

"Reckon he is," grunted the cowboy. In the meantime John Blevins, having seen the new sheriff ride down the street, rushed to warn Andy in the saloon where he was tossing down drinks. Andy told John to take a horse to the Blevins house—"just in case." Then he left the bar and walked into the street, his hand near the butt of his gun.

The Blevins house, a white frame, L-shaped building, was across the railroad tracks from the main part of town. As Andy Cooper walked toward the house, his eyes scanned the street in both directions. Several hundred feet away he could see the livery stable and he knew Sheriff Owens was there preparing for battle.

Windows in the short row of squat buildings along Holbrook's main street were lined with men waiting for the shooting to start. They watched Andy Cooper cross the tracks and disappear into the Blevins place. Then John Blevins rode up on a horse, tied it a few feet from the front porch, and followed Andy inside.

At the livery stable Commodore Owens examined his pistols and calmly removed his rifle from its saddle holster. This completed to his satisfaction, he walked slowly up the street to the town's only drug store. Inside he asked if anyone knew where Andy Cooper was hiding out.

"Just saw him go up to the Blevins place," said Mr. Watron, owner of the store and one of the few solid citizens of Holbrook.

"Thanks," said Owens. With his rifle under his arm, the sheriff started up the street—one man against an unknown number of armed killers.

The Blevins house had two front doors leading off the porch into a large living room. Owens knew he was being watched from the windows of both the ground and the second floors as he climbed the few steps to the porch floor. Reaching the door, he knocked softly. There was no answer. He knocked again, harder this time.

The door swung open a few inches and before him stood the wanted man, the forty-five in his right hand leveled straight at the sheriff's heart.

"Andy Cooper?" asked the sheriff, ignoring the gun in his face.

"That's me," Cooper replied. "What do you want?"

"I have a warrant for your arrest for stealing horses and I intend to take you in, Cooper."

Cooper's eyes flashed nervously. There was something about the man before him that told him he was facing a capable fighter. While he hesitated, wondering what to do, Owens heard the click of a gun behind him as the hammer was cocked for firing. It was Sam Blevins who had quietly emerged from the second door. He

covered Sheriff Owens point-blank from a distance of only a few feet.

Cooper broke the dread seconds of silence by shouting "I won't go!" and by simultaneously slamming the door as he pulled the trigger of his Colt forty-five.

Sheriff Owens went into action like a bolt of lightning. In a split second he kicked the door, throwing Cooper's aim off, he blasted Cooper through the closed door by firing the Winchester from his hip, and, leaping backwards, he threw his body off the porch to safety as Sam Blevins' bullet whizzed past his head.

Owens' second shot sent Sam Blevins spinning back into the house. His next shot caught Cooper, who had staggered to a window, revolver in hand, and dropped him to the floor—dead. For a second all was quiet except for the curses coming from the house. Commodore Perry Owens raced to a more protected position. Suddenly one of the doors flew open and out charged John Blevins, firing his gun desperately as he came. Owens raised his revolver and caught John in mid-air. He fell and never got up.

The sheriff's sharp eye caught a slight movement at the corner of one of the upstairs windows. Mose Roberts, a member of the Blevins clan by marriage, poked the barrel of his revolver through the glass pane. Owens fired again and Roberts fell to the floor.

Owens stood there motionless, waiting for the next figure to appear, but in less than one minute the battle was over. The house was silent except for the groans of the wounded. Commodore Perry Owens walked back through town, past the eyes peering at him in amazement and fury. The back of the Tewksbury-Graham feud was broken. A few days later he threw the warrant for the arrest of Andy Cooper on the county clerk's desk. Across the face of the warrant was written in the sheriff's hand: "Killed while resisting arrest."

Although Commodore Perry Owens worked alone and lacked the faculty of inspiring his deputies, his bravery was never questioned. His fight with Andy Cooper is one of the classic examples of a western peace officer at his best.

After a long life of thrilling adventures among bad men, outlaws, and Indians, Owens gave up the man-hunting business in 1900 and opened a store in Seligman, Arizona, where he died May 10, 1919, from natural causes—one of the few fighting sheriffs of early Arizona to survive those lawless days.

WILLIAM MULVENON

15.

WILLIAM MULVENON

THE SHERIFF WHO KEPT HIS HEAD THROUGHOUT
A BLOODY RANGE WAR

ONE OF THE most bitter range feuds the Old West ever knew was the Pleasant Valley war which swept through Arizona in the late 1880's. It was fought in defiance of the law until all of its participants had either been killed or had tired of the fight and put aside their arms. Officers of the law were unable to stop the bloodshed, though many a brave sheriff tried, and among these was Sheriff William Mulvenon of Yavapai County.

Pleasant Valley is entirely surrounded by mountains—tranquil, rugged, beautiful, but in the 1880's it was the most remote, wild, and lawless section of Arizona, the nearest white settlement more than a hundred miles away.

To the north the Mogollon Mountains formed a natural barrier through which only a few passes permitted the driving of livestock. It was the movement of a herd of sheep over the Mogollons by the Tewksburys that caused the Grahams to declare war.

John Tewksbury had come to Pleasant Valley from Boston by way of California. He married an Indian woman, who bore him three sons. Later, about the time he settled in Cherry Creek in Pleasant Valley, he married a woman of English birth. Old John Tewksbury never quarreled with anyone as he went about his business of raising cattle and hogs.

Tom and John Graham were from Iowa, and

they, too, came to Arizona after first trying their luck in the gold fields of California. They built a cabin about ten miles from Tewksbury's and also began raising cattle.

Occasionally there had been some trouble between the Grahams and the Tewksburys over missing cattle, and each had accused the other side of rustling. Still, there was no bloodshed, and the valley did not yet resound to the crack of gunfire.

Atop the Mogollon rim the Daggs brothers grazed many sheep, but in wintertime the ranges were snow covered and the sheep had a tough struggle to survive. Below the rim, in Pleasant Valley, the buffalo grass was knee high and well protected from winter storms. The Daggs wanted to winter their sheep herds in Pleasant Valley, but knew that to do so would probably mean war with both the Grahams and the Tewksburys. War alone was too much for them to handle, so they considered taking on one family as allies against the other. Carefully the Daggs approached the Tewksburys with a proposal to share the profits from the sheep in return for the right to graze in Pleasant Valley and for armed intervention against the Grahams if they dared object.

The Grahams could hardly believe their eyes when they saw sheep pouring down the rim of the Mogollons and, riding with the herd, their rifles ready for action, John Tewksbury's three half-Indian boys.

The Grahams drew the first blood by killing a sheepherder. From that moment on, the valley was in flames and other settlers were drawn into the fight. Allied with the Grahams were Mart Blevins and his five sons, including the cold-blooded killer, Andy Cooper.

Following the shooting of the Navajo sheepherder, which was not of sufficient importance to command the attention of a busy peace officer, it was only a question of time before white men would be killing each other. The first pitched battle occurred at the ranch cabin of William Middleton when the Tewksburys opened fire on a Graham party, killing two men and seriously wounding another.

When news of the killings reached Sheriff William Mulvenon at Prescott, he secured ten arrest warrants for the Tewksburys and set out for Pleasant Valley with a hard-riding posse. Finding the Tewksbury ranches deserted, some

of them burned to the ground, they decided that the men had fled temporarily to the mountains. Attempts to follow their trail failed and Sheriff Mulvenon returned to Prescott. With the departure of the sheriff's forces from Pleasant Valley, hostilities flared up again and Andy Cooper swore to drive every Tewksbury out of the valley or to kill them trying.

The Graham forces, with as many as twenty armed men in the valley at most times, rode through the country and drove the Tewksburys into the brush like hunted rabbits.

Young William Graham was ambushed on a lonely trail and killed by a deputy sheriff from Apache County, who was fighting on the side of the Tewksburys. A few weeks later the Grahams found a party of the Tewksburys reoccupying one of their former cabins. They blocked every exit and poured lead through the walls of the building. Young John Tewksbury and William Jacobs tried to reach their horses and were dropped in their tracks. The siege lasted all day, but the Grahams were un-

able to account for more of their enemies and finally rode away, firing one last volley into the little cabin.

Two days later Sheriff Commodore Perry Owens walked up to the Blevins home in Holbrook, attempted to arrest Andy Cooper, and killed three of the Graham supporters in the few seconds' gun battle that followed.

After Commodore Perry Owens reduced the Grahams' numbers, the remaining Tewksburys came down from their mountain hideouts to renew the fight. More men were killed and once more Pleasant Valley flared into open warfare.

Having been openly defied once by the feudists, Sheriff Bill Mulvenon decided that there was but one thing to do to end the bitter range war—ride into the valley with a posse large enough to arrest all the fighters, even if it meant killing them to subdue them. He determined to round up the Grahams first, although it was never quite clear why.

About twenty men, each sworn to secrecy, rode into the valley behind Billy Mulvenon. They placed everyone they encountered on the trip to the battle grounds under arrest so that word of the invasion could not be carried to the Grahams in advance of the posse.

Twelve days after riding out of Prescott, the posse reached the Graham ranch where part of the Graham faction was believed to be in hiding. The men carefully hid their horses in the brush and before daylight they secreted themselves behind the Perkins store, which was in sight of the Graham ranch. Then, in an effort to lead the Grahams into the ambush, six members of the posse rode casually past the Graham cabin and tied their horses at the Perkins store while they went inside as if everything was as usual. It was felt that while the Grahams would not openly fight twenty men, they would not hesitate to take on six.

During a considerable wait no action came from the Graham ranch, so Mulvenon ordered the six riders to mount and ride away. This trick worked. Presently two gun shots came from the Graham headquarters, apparently to signal that all was clear, for the ranch became a beehive of activity. Two men, John Graham and Charles Blevins, mounted their horses and rode toward the Perkins store. They approached the store cautiously, started to circle it, and came in sight of the concealed posse. Sheriff Mulvenon stood with a shotgun raised to his shoulder.

"Put up your hands!" commanded the sheriff. The two surprised riders wheeled their horses and reached for their six-shooters. It was an instant too late. Mulvenon and the posse opened fire, and the two men fell from their bolting horses—Graham dead and Blevins dying.

Mulvenon and the posse, aware that the remaining Grahams in the cabin had heard the gunfire, hurriedly surrounded the spot and captured Al Rose. Tom Graham, the only remaining member of the clan in the cabin, managed to sneak out and make his escape. The posse then rode to the Tewksbury headquarters and captured five of the rival clan without a fight.

From then on the Graham-Tewksbury feud became a little less bloody, but it flared up from time to time. Of the three Graham brothers, only Tom had survived the shooting from ambush, the planned attacks, and the accidental pitched battles. Of the fighting Blevins family, five of the six men were dead and the other was in jail. The Tewksburys had fared little better.

But now that the law had finally dared to enter Pleasant Valley and break up the feud, the brave work of Sheriff William Mulvenon was partially undone by the feeble courts. All of the captured participants in the fight were released on bond and eventually dismissed.

The job of keeping the peace in a flaming war of hatred such as existed between the hard-shooting Grahams and the quick-triggered Tewksburys fell upon the shoulders of one man —William Mulvenon. By today's standards of law enforcement, he would have been accused of neglect of duty because of his slowness to act at the start of the feud, but his level head prevailed in a day when guns were drawn at the slightest provocation and he helped to prevent further bloodshed in Pleasant Valley.

JIM ROBERTS

JIM ROBERTS

16.

JIM ROBERTS

THE MARSHAL WHO COULD FIGHT OLD STYLE

OR MODERN STYLE

JIM ROBERTS was a deputy sheriff, sheriff, constable, and marshal for nearly fifty years, and one of the very few old-time peace officers of the frontier West to survive the hectic, reckless days of gun law.

During his years as a member of the feuding clan of Tewksburys in the Pleasant Valley war in Arizona and later as a peace officer, he killed more men than he could remember, but his aging hands were still steady with a gun as late as 1928 when he killed the outlaw Bill Forrester during a bank holdup at Clarkdale.

James Franklin Roberts was born in Missouri in 1858, and from the start the love of adven-

ture was in his blood. By the time he was a young man and out in the world on his own, he had found the raw life of Arizona exactly suited to him.

After wandering around Arizona's rough mining camps and cow towns for a few years he found a spot in Pleasant Valley that offered fine possibilities for a horse ranch. Here Jim built a cabin and settled down to raising fancy horses, for which he soon became noted.

In the rugged and lawless land of that day, Jim Roberts expected to lose a few horses to thieves now and then. When these losses became too great, however, Jim looked around for the

103

culprits and finally decided that some of the Graham-Blevins clan were raiding his stock. It was probably the day he caught one of the Graham cowboys red-handed that he made the decision to ride with the Tewksburys, but it was not until he found his cabin in smoking ruins some time later that he actually swore to exterminate as many Grahams as possible. He turned out to be the Tewksburys' hardest riding and fastest shooting member.

After the Pleasant Valley war died down, Jim Roberts, like most of the clan's fighting cronies, was broke. He drifted into the booming copper camp of Congress City and, because of his fighting reputation, was appointed a deputy sheriff by Bucky O'Neill in 1889—the start of a long and honorable career as a peace officer. Two years later he was appointed full sheriff. After serving for one year he accepted an appointment as constable for the entire Jerome mining district.

As constable of the Jerome district, Jim Roberts had little real authority to control the lawlessness that was slowly engulfing the mining capital of Jerome, one of the last strongholds of the bad men who were being pushed out of other areas. The city fathers of Jerome looked around for a real fighting city marshal and offered the job to several men who turned it down as being too tough.

When the job was held out to Jim Roberts in 1904, he knew it was one of the few really tough places in the West, and a job for a full-size fighting man. He accepted.

Roberts set out to show the bad men who was going to have the upper hand in Jerome, but before he could convince them that it was to be Marshal Roberts, several of them had to be killed. After that, Jerome was a right peaceful town.

A quiet town never appealed to a peace officer of Jim Roberts' temperament, and, when Jerome tamed down, Roberts moved to the near-by camp of Clarkdale as a special officer with a sheriff's commission for the United Verde Copper Company, which virtually owned Clarkdale.

In the course of his duties at Jerome and Clarkdale, Jim Roberts saw the wild and woolly West turn into a land as peaceful as any section of the country, with only an occasional outlaw turning up to break the monotony of a quiet mining camp. Two of these latter-day outlaws were Bill Forrester and Earl Nelson who had teamed up in Kansas and decided to pick up some easy money in Arizona. It was in 1928 that the two men drifted into Clarkdale. Forrester found a job driving a stage for the company hospital; Nelson went to work in a garage, for the automobile had now invaded the Southwest.

The two outlaws looked around for an easy killing and selected Clarkdale's Bank of Arizona. If they had ever heard of Clarkdale's Jim Roberts, they pretended not to be impressed by his reputation as a gun fighter and they went ahead, laying their plans with care. Their escape automobile was loaded with many cans of roofing nails to be scattered on the highway as they speeded away, in order to stop pursuit by car. For the benefit of any bloodhounds that might be brought in to trail them if they had to take to the mountains, quantities of pepper and oil of peppermint were cached in the car, along with a formidable arsenal of guns and a vast supply of food.

On the morning of June 21, they strolled into the bank and quickly covered the two bank employees and thirteen customers. Scooping $50,-000 into a sack, they shoved the fifteen people into the vault and closed the huge door upon them.

Old Jim Roberts, on the job as he had been for so many years, was strolling down the street when he saw two men dash out of the Bank of Arizona, one carrying a sack and both brandishing guns. They jumped into the waiting car and roared away, with the old marshal firing at them. Nor had Jim Roberts, in spite of age, lost any of his deadliness with a gun. One shot from his old single-action Colt six gun crashed into Bill Forrester's head. He was at the wheel of the speeding car, which rammed headlong into the stone wall of a building under construction. A telephone pole guy wire ripped the top from the open car.

Nelson jumped from the wreckage, his gun spitting lead at the special officer. Jim Roberts, who had stood up to the deadliest fighting men in frontier Arizona, was not about to be chased to cover by a modern-day bandit. He had been under fire too many times and, when Nelson turned to run, old Jim Roberts ran in pursuit.

In spite of their well-laid plans and the mountain of ammunition in the wrecked car, Nelson ran out of cartridges and had to surrender or be killed. Jim Roberts brought his men to heel—one dead, the other completely cowed. For an old peace officer who should have been in retirement, it was a phenomenal feat—dropping a man with a shot in the head as he crouched over the wheel of a speeding automobile!

Jim Roberts had spent nearly fifty years as a peace officer after serving as the fightingest member of a lawless clan in a lawless country, but even then, he was fighting for what he thought was justice—the right to raise fine horses without losing them to thieves.

He died with his boots on in January 1934 at the age of seventy-five from heart trouble, not the outlaw's bullet that put an end to so many Western peace officers. Few men living at that time could look back upon more adventure-packed years in the Old West of Indians, outlaws, and rustlers than Jim Roberts.

GLENN REYNOLDS AND THE APACHE KID

17.

GLENN REYNOLDS
AND THE APACHE KID

GLENN REYNOLDS was the hard-shooting sheriff of Gila County, Arizona, during the days when the warlike Apaches were still a dangerous threat to early settlers and the Army and local peace officers alike were busy keeping the Indians in check.

Reynolds had lived the usual life of the frontiersman, coming west as a young man, riding the range, and fighting outlaws and highwaymen. It was his fate to meet up with one of the cleverest of the Apaches, who were well known for their trickery.

In 1872 the Army was engaged in rounding up the scattered Apaches and locating them on reservations. The Indians headed for the brush like quail where the scouts and the soldiers had to trail them down.

One day a sergeant named Clay Beauford overtook a family of Apaches, one of whom was a small urchin, the son of a chief and heir to his father's position. The family was brought into the agency at San Carlos and the boy, known only as "the Kid," attached himself to Beauford's group of soldiers. He haunted the camp and, no matter what the soldiers did, there was no getting rid of him. They finally adopted him as their mascot.

One day Beauford had to dismiss one of his Indian scouts for some offense, and the Kid, now a young man, wiry and bold, quick as lightning and cunning as a fox, was offered the position. The Kid expressed his delight for, although he spoke only the Apache language, Beauford could converse with him.

Short and stocky, knowing every detail of the Apache country and the intimate ways of his people, the Kid became an excellent scout and a commendable soldier. There was one thing, however, that worried him. His father, who was a prominent chief, had been killed in a fight with another Indian, and the tribal law of the Apaches demanded that the Kid avenge his death by taking the life of his killer. When the Kid asked permission to leave the reservation to look for the man who had killed his father, he was refused. Slipping away, he recruited a small band of Indians, tracked down the killer, and slew him.

Upon his return to the agency, the Kid was placed under arrest. He and his followers revolted and fired on the soldiers, badly injuring Al Sieber, one of the Army's most famous scouts. In the confusion, the Kid recovered his carbine, jumped on a horse and, followed by a few friends, escaped into Mexico. On the way they killed at least two white men.

The escaping Indians were hotly pursued, but they cleverly doubled back in their tracks to the reservation from which they had escaped, where they were hidden and fed by a few Apache friends. After much dickering five of the Indians, including the Kid, surrendered. They were tried and sentenced to various terms of imprisonment at Alcatraz in California.

The following year the President of the United States ordered the five Apaches released from prison and retried. The Indians were returned to the San Carlos Reservation. In October 1889, they were taken into Globe and tried a second time. The Kid, who had been such a favorite with the soldiers, was found guilty of assaulting Sieber and was sentenced to ten years in the Territorial Prison at Yuma, a walled bake-

oven in the boiling sun on the banks of the Colorado River.

A few weeks later Sheriff Glenn Reynolds was ordered to take the Kid and eight other prisoners —seven Indians and a Mexican—from Globe to Yuma. He was accompanied by one guard and

make a break. Reynolds was walking on ahead, while Holmes brought up the rear. Suddenly, at a pre-arranged signal, the Indians nearest the sheriff and the guard gave a war whoop and attacked the two men with their free arms. They succeeded in getting the officers' guns and,

the driver of the four-horse stage in which the prisoners rode. Reynolds rode on horseback behind the stage as far as Riverside, where they stayed all night.

On the following morning it was quite cold and both Reynolds and Holmes, the guard, wore heavy coats and gloves. Both rode on the stage, making twelve passengers in all—a heavy load for the four horses.

About five miles out of Riverside the stage reached a grade, and Reynolds ordered the Indians to walk while the stage negotiated the steep climb.

Although the prisoners were handcuffed in pairs, they were on the lookout for a chance to

while some covered the stage, the others proceeded to kill Reynolds and Holmes.

Sheriff Glenn Reynolds was shot with the rifle taken from Holmes, receiving a shotgun blast in the head that killed him instantly. To show their hatred of Reynolds, the Indians then beat him with the rifle butt and threw stones at the body. The stage driver turned just in time to get a bullet in the cheek. He fell from the stage and feigned death. The Indians robbed him and left him for dead. After the prisoners had fled, he recovered and made his way back to Riverside to spread the tragic news.

A posse followed the trail of the fleeing Indians, and soldiers scoured the area. It was a fruitless search. The Indians had somehow managed to free themselves of their handcuffs and, splitting up, disappeared into the desert. During the next two or three years the fugitives drifted back to the reservation at San Carlos one by one and were hidden by their people. The Apache Kid, however, turned savage. He wandered along the border, killing people once in a while, and probably getting credit for many he did not kill. Even with a reward of five thousand dollars on his head, the soldiers found him impossible to track down.

In 1893 the Kid turned up on the San Carlos Reservation, stole the young wife of a prominent Apache, and immediately disappeared. A group of Apaches were permitted to take up his trail, but so cunning was the Kid that even the best trackers among his own people found it impossible to trail him.

The Kid frequently returned to the reservation, where he recruited followers and usually managed to get away with a young squaw.

It was later learned that the Kid had a hideout high on a mountain where, with a powerful telescope he had stolen, he was able to watch the country for miles around. When he saw a solitary cattleman or prospector, it was his custom to lie in ambush behind a rock or other protection, shoot the man from behind, and rob the body. With the aid of his telescope, he could keep far ahead of his pursuers when he was closely pressed.

In the rocky country in which the Kid traveled, he was able to move about without leaving a sign of a trail behind him. He was an expert at wood and field craft, and he kept both Indians and whites in such fear of him that they would neither hunt him nor report any of his activities. He used the squaws he stole as servants, to gather his food, to cook for him, to stand guard, and even to fight for him if necessary.

After the late 1890's, the Kid was never seen again in Arizona. Probably due to the price on his head, to the constant influx of settlers, and to the firm conviction that his luck would one day run out, he got out of the state. He may have gone to Mexico where he is thought to have married into a Yaqui family. Here he is said to have organized bands of Indians who raided Mexican villages, but always managed to escape into the mountains.

Whatever the mystery surrounding the Apache Kid, the fact remains that he led a charmed life in avoiding capture so many years. With his departure the Apache depredations of Arizona ended and the regime of law and order, started by men like Sheriff Glenn Reynolds, became a reality.

SHERIFF JACK HAYS
AND THE SYDNEY DUCKS

SHERIFF JACK HAYS
AND THE SYDNEY DUCKS

18.

SHERIFF JACK HAYS
AND THE SYDNEY DUCKS

SHERIFF JACK HAYS was one of the first peace officers of the West to try his hand at keeping law and order in a full-fledged city—and the fine reputation he had earned as a Texas Ranger suffered from the day he was elected sheriff of the roaring new city of San Francisco on the West Coast.

John C. Hays had started life far to the east in Tennessee. Shortly after moving to Texas to settle in San Antonio, he joined the Texas Rangers in time to take part in a battle with the Comanche Indians on Plum Creek in 1840. Before the year was out he had distinguished himself as a fighter to the point of becoming a captain. In the following year singlehanded he killed ten Indians in a fierce fight in Uvalde

Canyon. For this daring piece of devotion to duty he was made a major.

One of the most famous Texas Rangers, Hays had the reputation of never turning back once he started after a band of Indians or headed out on the trail of an outlaw. Armed with a rifle, a pistol and a knife, with a Mexican blanket tied across his saddle, and carrying a little salt, some ammunition, and perhaps a small tin of parched corn, he could ride for weeks. Forced to sleep in the open much of the time and traveling days away from even the smallest settlement, a Texas Ranger had to be good to subsist—and there is no doubt that Jack Hays was one of the best.

When the Mexican War broke out, Hays

could not resist getting a piece of that action. He served the country with credit, coming out of the war a colonel.

Then in April 1850, the city of San Francisco, a bustling center of miner's outfitters, saloons, gambling dens, and wooden ships, was incorporated and elected its first city officials. Colonel John C. Hays was chosen sheriff of the new city. In accepting the job he had no idea that he was finally getting more action than he could handle. His job was to control a wholly unfamiliar type of bad man, the city criminal, furtive and lacking even the vestiges of honor that distinguished the desperadoes in the cow towns and railheads farther to the east.

Along with the thousands of adventurers who had thronged to San Francisco in the gold rush, there had come a horde of criminals—pickpockets, thugs, murderers, and gangsters, who had not the slightest intention of working in the mines or any place else. Among them were many released criminals from Australia, who lived in tents or wooden shacks on the edge of the city. They organized themselves into a band known as the Sydney Ducks and were among the most active in robbing miners in the dark streets and waylaying unwary patrons of the crowded bars and gambling halls.

Soon they became so bold in their outrages that honest citizens were afraid to go out at night. Within a few months, more than one hundred people had been murdered. The Sydney Ducks were even accused of setting some of the many fires that burned the city in the early days.

Local law officers were apparently helpless when it came to capturing the killers, and when

they did catch any, the courts seemed reluctant to punish them. It was impossible to find a witness to a crime, for if one appeared, defense attorneys delayed the trial until he could be killed.

When Jack Hays was appointed sheriff, the solider citizens breathed a sigh of relief. Hays would surely be the end of the Ducks! Why, an old Texas Ranger and Indian fighter like him would clean them out in no time at all! But after several months of Jack Hays's inaction, the citizens began to wonder if the new sheriff was going to get down to business. They wanted action—and quick!

Finally after a score of major crimes were committed in a single night, about two hundred citizens joined together and formed a vigilante committee with a constitution and bylaws, which they had published in the local news-

papers, frowning upon the secrecy usually sought by most such committees. Two strokes upon a bell, repeated every minute was the signal for the two hundred members to gather at their assembly room.

On the very night the constitution was adopted and signed, two members of the Vigilantes caught one of the Ducks, John Jenkins, a man with a bad reputation in both Australia and this country, in the act of stealing a safe. The prisoner was hauled into the meeting place and someone struck the bell twice with a club. From all over San Francisco the Vigilante mem-

bers gathered. A trial was held immediately and John Jenkins, caught in the act as he had certainly been, was found guilty. The penalty was

death and the sentence was carried out immediately at the old adobe Customs House in the Plaza.

Although the law enforcement officers of San Francisco frowned upon a group of men taking the maintenance of order into their own hands, the citizens generally agreed that this was the only kind of action that would frighten the thugs and murderers into leaving for other parts.

Organization of the Vigilantes continued on a very businesslike basis, and their numbers increased tremendously. Specific duties were assigned to the members. Some were instructed to investigate the gambling halls and to list those places harboring criminals. Others were to watch the incoming ships in order to prevent known criminals from landing. Detailed records were kept of every activity.

Without waiting for investigation, many of the criminals suddenly disappeared into the mining camps of the gold fields, but there were still some who challenged the committee's authority and refused to go. Among these was a boy of sixteen, James Stuart, who had been banished from England to Australia for forgery and had made his way to San Francisco about 1850. Stuart was known to be a horse thief, a robber, and a burglar. One night he killed a merchant in one of the mining camps in an attempted robbery.

Although a man answering Stuart's description was arrested and convicted, some of the Vigilantes learned that the real Stuart was still free. Finally the committee caught Stuart. An attorney friend of Stuart's secured a writ of habeas corpus, and Sheriff Jack Hayes was ordered to get Stuart from the Vigilantes and bring him into court.

While it was Hays's duty to see that the orders of the court were carried out, he found reasons to delay serving the writ. This gave the Vigilantes time to act. The bell was struck, and some nine hundred Vigilantes appeared for the trial of James Stuart. Again the verdict was guilty and the lad was marched through the streets to the Market Street wharf where eager hands strung him to a beam.

Even though young Stuart had confessed the crimes charged to him, the courts cried out against a band of men taking the law into their own hands. A grand jury indicted the Vigilantes, but peace officers refused to arrest them, and the jury resigned in disgust.

By this time the outrages committed in other places by the gangs fleeing from San Francisco led to the formation of vigilante committees in Sacramento, Marysville, Stockton, and other towns. In Monterey Sheriff Hearne captured two of the worst of the Ducks, Sam Whittaker and Robert McKenzie. He promptly took them to San Francisco and turned them over to the Vigilantes who locked them up. It was generally known around San Francisco that they were to be hanged.

When Governor McDougal heard that Whittaker and McKenzie were to be hanged on the following day, he hurried to San Francisco and went into conference with the mayor. Late in the morning a judge was found who agreed to issue a writ for the prisoner's release. Sheriff Jack Hays was roused from bed to serve the writ and secure the two prisoners.

Hays, having no choice, went to the committee headquarters with a deputy and had little trouble in talking the guards out of releasing the Australians.

The Vigilantes, fearing the men would be freed by the courts, sent a delegation to invite Sheriff Hays to attend a bullfight the next day at the Mission Dolores. While the sheriff was enjoying the hospitality of the committee at the fights, another group of twenty-nine men forced their way into the jail and seized Whittaker and McKenzie.

Again the alarm was struck on the bell and a crowd gathered on Battery Street where two gallows were speedily erected. Asserting that the Australians were confessed criminals, the Vigilantes led them to the dangling ropes and soon nooses tightened around their necks.

With the double hanging of Whittaker and McKenzie, the remaining members of the Sydney Ducks left San Francisco and were never heard of again. Slowly the Vigilante Committee turned over the maintenance of law and order to duly elected officers.

Sheriff Jack Hays served out his term and retired. Whereas as a Texas Ranger he had been in complete control of the border outlaws, he was not up to the job of controlling a gang of city toughs in a teeming gold-crazy age. It was not that Jack Hays lacked courage, for he had proved that in Texas. He simply could not understand a criminal who struck in the dark and disappeared until ready for his next crime. It was his misfortune to be an old-fashioned peace officer pitted against the wily urban criminal.

FRANK CANTON

FRANK CANTON

19.

FRANK CANTON

BORDER-TO-BORDER PEACE OFFICER

Frank Canton was a tall, fearless, arrogant man, a dead shot, and as tough and hard as the outlaws and rustlers he chased. He risked his own life with the same reckless abandon with which he took other lives. Some say he brought peace to the eastern grazing lands of Wyoming, but others claim he served the powerful cattle barons in their attempt to drive out the homesteaders and the little cattlemen. Whatever the case, Frank Canton was a true frontiersman and a fighting peace officer who loved action more than anything else.

For more than fifty years Canton served as a Texas Ranger, U.S. deputy marshal, sheriff, live-

stock inspector, and secret service man, and his trail stretched from Mexico to Alaska. His real name was not Frank Canton, but it was the only name he ever used since leaving his Texas home two steps ahead of the law as a boy.

Frank Canton was born in Virginia in 1849. While he was still a child, his parents moved to the great open plains of northern Texas, where a man had to be tough to survive. It was a country of vast rolling prairies where countless thousands of wild cattle and buffalo roamed and where the few white settlements lived in constant fear of Indian attacks—the land of the cowboy and the haven of the desperado.

121

From the time Frank was big enough to sit in a saddle, he was riding the range, associating with cowboys and bad men, learning to use a rope and a gun. When he was seventeen, he was as tough as nails and eager to join one of the great cattle drives northward to Kansas or Nebraska. There was no bigger adventure for a boy who craved for action and excitement.

Canton joined a trail outfit taking a herd of fifteen hundred cattle to the wild cow town of Abilene, Kansas. Cattle drives were frequently ordeals of extreme hardship, and Canton's first would have finished a lad made of lesser stuff. Electric storms stampeded the cattle in the dead of night. Heavy rains turned the prairies to quagmires and flooded the streams to raging torrents. Indians dogged their trail and stole stray cattle. Outlaws and rustlers were a constant threat, and after the rains, the prairie sun boiled down furiously. After four months and more than a thousand miles of danger and peril, the cattle were delivered and young Frank Canton could rightfully call himself a man.

Back in Texas and itching for more action, Canton joined the famous Texas Rangers, one of the bravest and grandest peace organizations ever to patrol the plains of the West. A Ranger had to be a bronco buster, an expert with a rope, an unexcelled gunman, and a man capable of enduring untold hardships. More than that, he had to live by the ideals of justice and fair play. The life of a Ranger was a constant battle with Indians and outlaws, horse thieves and cattle rustlers.

When Texas tamed down, Canton sought more exciting country and again joined a cattle drive to the north. After delivering the herd in Ogallala, Nebraska, he accepted a position with the Wyoming Stock Raisers Association as field inspector, working out of Cheyenne but ranging northwest to the Yellowstone country and into Montana. His duties were to track down criminals, protect the ranchers, recover stolen cattle, and supply evidence against stock thieves.

In 1880 Frank Canton moved to Buffalo, Wyoming, and commenced farming and stock raising although he was still employed by the Stock Association. Buffalo was in Johnson County, an immense area covering almost half the present state where there was intense rivalry between the small pioneer homesteaders and the big cattle kings for the rich grasslands of the country.

Frank Canton was elected sheriff of Johnson County in 1882. With one of the largest groups of deputies in the West, he spent most of his time in the saddle, running down cattle thieves, stage robbers, and rustlers. One of the many outlaws Canton captured was Teton Jackson, a burly giant who operated a gang of thieves out of the famous Jackson Hole County in western Wyoming. Jackson was imprisoned, but he escaped, leaving behind a note with the names of the men he intended to kill. Frank Canton's name headed the list.

After serving as sheriff for two terms, Canton declined to run for a third and retired to his ranch. The Johnson County cattle war was shaping up, however, and Frank Canton was not the type of man who would or could keep out of it.

The West generally made its own laws, and in most instances the party with the most gun power forced its ideas of law upon the others. In Wyoming the big cattlemen represented the law, and anyone crossing their path usually got the worst of it. The little fellows—the homesteaders, or the "nesters" as they were called—fenced in their ranges, interfering with the grazing of the big herds. They rebelled against the authority of the big cattle outfits, and the big outfits declared war. Who was right or who was wrong hasn't yet been settled, but many men on both sides paid with their lives for their part in the costly fight. The big cattlemen declared the small homesteaders to be rustlers, horse thieves, and outlaws and prepared a list of those to be killed. They then hired killers to do the job, to whom they handed over the "Dead List" of ranchers and farmers who dared to build fences on their own land.

At the start of the cattle war, Frank Canton was ranching and also serving as a deputy U.S. marshal and as an investigator for the Wyoming Stock Association, representing the big cattle interests.

In 1891 two small homesteaders, Ranger
Jones and John Tisdale, were ambushed and
killed. These were not the first killings, but they
aroused the small ranchers, who organized their
own stock association in open defiance of the
powerful cattlemen. At the same time the new
association accused Frank Canton of killing
Jones and Tisdale. Things got so hot that Canton found it convenient to leave the country for
a spell.

Canton later joined forces with, and commanded for a while an armed band of hired
killers sent into Johnson County to clean out
the homesteaders under the pretext that they
were rustlers. A battle resulted in which two of
the homesteaders and one of the invaders were
killed. The remaining homesteaders dug in at
Buffalo and prepared for a long siege. Just as
the battle was about to start, U.S. Army soldiers
arrived to break up the fight. The cattle war was
over.

Canton was not welcome in parts of Wyoming. Until things quieted down, he took a position as superintendent of a packing plant in
Nebraska City. This kind of a job was bound to
bore a man of Canton's type, however, and he
resigned to go to Oklahoma, then Indian Territory and a rendezvous for the worst gangs of

outlaws in the Southwest. In the frontier town of Pawnee as under-sheriff and deputy U.S. marshal he set out to break up such famous gangs of desperados as the Daltons and the Doolins.

lar's worth of gold dust as it was packed out of the country for shipment to Seattle.

In the summer of 1899, Canton tired of Alaska and returned to Oklahoma where he had a job in the sheriff's office in Comanche County.

After several years of strenuous work in Oklahoma, Frank Canton again was off for new lands and new adventures. Many thousands of men were flocking into Alaska and the big stampede was on to the Klondike district. Canton secured an appointment as deputy U.S. marshal for the Interior of Alaska. His first winter in Alaska was spent in prospecting, although there were frequent trips to round up a criminal or to recover stolen property. On one occasion Canton guarded a shipment of over a million dollar's worth of gold dust as it was packed out of the country for shipment to Seattle.

Later he went to work for the Cattle Raisers Association of Texas, in charge of the criminal work on the range.

When Oklahoma was admitted as a state, Canton was appointed Adjutant General of the Oklahoma National Guard, in which capacity he served for nine years. When death claimed him in 1927, he had spent practically all of fifty years as a peace officer with one title or another, and his restless feet had taken him across most of the frontier trails of Western America.

HENRY PLUMMER

20.

HENRY PLUMMER

THE SHERIFF WHO HUNG FROM HIS OWN GALLOWS

MOST WESTERN peace officers upheld what dignity there was in the job of riding herd on outlaws and Indians in a respectable manner. There were others, however, who were out for all they could get while apparently preserving peace and order. Henry Plummer of Montana was of the latter ilk.

Thoroughly lacking in moral courage, Henry Plummer used his office to enrich himself and the gang he built around him. He betrayed, robbed, and killed the people he was sworn to protect and turned the sheriff's job into one of scorn and hatred. He corrupted a whole community until a handful of honest citizens took matters into their own hands and hanged the sheriff from the very gallows he had built for the execution of his political enemies.

Plummer migrated from the east to California in 1852. In the following summer he and a partner opened a bakery in the mining camp of Nevada City. A few years later he was elected marshal of the town, but before the expiration of his term, he killed a man in an argument over a woman. He was convicted and sent to prison, but was pardoned in a few months.

Returning to Nevada City, Plummer soon killed another man. Forced to leave the community, he joined up with a band of stagecoach robbers. The bitterness against him in Nevada City did not prevent him from returning later to kill still another man. He was jailed, but a friend smuggled two pistols to him, and he fought his way to freedom.

Plummer moved on to other parts. In the

spring of 1861 he was operating a gambling table in Lewiston, Idaho, while secretly working with a gang of horse thieves and stage robbers on the side. Before long Plummer was at the head of the outlaw band, directing their activities from town where he pretended to be a respectable citizen. After killing a man for calling him a coward, he moved his gang headquarters to Florence.

In the fall of 1862, three of Plummer's men were dragged from jail, where they had been lodged for holding up a pack train, and hanged. Henry Plummer moved on to the booming camp of Bannack, Montana, the chief center of placer gold mining on the eastern slopes of the Rockies.

A year later there was a city election, and in some undetermined manner Henry Plummer, the killer, was elected sheriff. Perhaps he won the election because, only in his late twenties, he was a handsome man and he could make an excellent impression on strangers if he wished to do so. At the time of his election, he already had a bandit system set up. Operating out of their headquarters at Rattlesnake Ranch, the

bandits spread a reign of terror over most of southwestern Montana.

Wearing the sheriff's badge in Bannack, of course, placed Plummer above suspicion, and it was much easier to operate now without fear of being caught. With spies in practically every

saloon and store, and a hundred or more road agents operating on the mountain trails, it was practically impossible for anyone to travel without being robbed by Plummer's gang.

So vast was the gang in numbers that a sailor's knot in a neckerchief was worn by each man so that they would not rob each other, and so extensive was the organization that secret marks were placed on stagecoaches carrying gold shipments to assure a profitable return for their effort and the risks they ran.

Once Plummer left Bannack for a few days to get married. During his absence he named three of his toughest and boldest bandits as his

deputies to take charge of the sheriff's office. To allay possible suspicion, he also deputized a respectable citizen, D. H. Dillingham.

Dillingham learned that the deputies planned the robbery of a friend and tipped him off. When the robbery failed to come off as planned, the deputies were so enraged that they killed Dillingham. A hastily formed vigilante committee erected gallows and set out to hang the three bandit-deputies, but at the last moment a faked letter arrived asserting their innocence. In the confusion, the killers escaped.

In the next few months Plummer strengthened his gang even more by recruiting miners who were down on their luck and promising them big rewards. To turn down his proposals meant death or an immediate departure from the country.

The two-faced sheriff himself took part in many holdups. To account for his absence, he resorted to many tricks, one of which was to have one of his men, dressed as a prospector, ride into town and demand that the sheriff accompany him to his diggings to settle an argument. On other occasions he would have a fake warrant brought to him and ride off into the hills to make an arrest.

When Plummer attempted to have himself appointed deputy U.S. marshal for the district, he ran into the Commissioner of the Territory, N. P. Langford, who suspected the sheriff of not being everything he seemed. Langford refused to recommend Plummer for the job, and the sheriff thereupon tried to have him killed, but with no success.

Sooner or later someone was bound to uncover the truth, and the first to actually do so was a lad named Henry Tilden. He was riding into Bannack when a group of horsemen approached him from ambush and robbed him. Henry Plummer was riding with the gang that day and, when his mask slipped down slightly, young Tilden was positive he recognized the face of the Bannack sheriff. He rode into town on a dead run and spread the news, which was not too amazing to some people who had begun to wonder about the lawlessness in Sheriff Plummer's and surrounding counties. For his own safety, Tilden was told by wise counselors to keep quiet or his life wouldn't be worth a wooden nickel.

By a strange coincidence, on the previous night young Tilden's uncle, Colonel Wilbur Sanders, had seen with his own eyes things that led him to believe that Plummer was really a bandit leader wearing a sheriff's badge. He had heard that Plummer and his deputies were packing ready to leave town. Suspecting that

they were going into the newly opened silver field to stake out claims for themselves, Sanders asked to be taken along. Plummer denied that they were going to the silver mines, stating that they were riding to Rattlesnake Ranch to make an arrest. No, Sanders had no business trailing along with the posse. This did not quite satisfy the Colonel. That night he rode secretly to the ranch and failed to locate Plummer or any of the party leaving Bannack with him. But Sanders did overhear some conversation that convinced him that Henry Plummer was actually head of the gang of road agents. He rode full speed back to Bannack, arriving about the same time as young Tilden, his nephew.

The stunning news started a whispering campaign, but Plummer remained in power because most people were afraid to bring the facts out into the open.

Plummer's chief deputy was a gay young killer named George Ives, who had come from a good Wisconsin family and operated a livery stable in near-by Virginia City. Ives's record of killings almost equaled that of his boss. After sizing up travelers for the amount of money they carried, he casually inquired the destination of those who seemed most affluent. They, of course, would be ambushed and robbed. Eventually word got around that people who put up at the Ives Livery Stable were usually robbed. The Ives place became very unpopular, and one man, suspecting the truth, threatened to expose Ives. A few days later his body was found by a hunter and taken into Nevada City, another near-by mining camp, where it caused great excitement and bitter feeling against George Ives.

A group of about twenty-five outraged citizens banded together and decided to do something to halt the robbers. That night they rode to George Ives's ranch and arrested him. Ives denied the killing, of course, but after a trial in which he was allowed to defend himself, he

was judged guilty and sentenced to hang. He pleaded to be tried in Bannack, where he was certain Sheriff Plummer would control the vigilante court, but the Nevada City people, already suspecting that Plummer was really the power behind the bandit gangs, refused.

Four days before Christmas a rope was placed around the neck of George Ives as he stood on a dry goods box suspended beneath a tripod made of three pine logs. The box was shot from under him and he plunged to his death, the first of the Plummer gang to be brought to justice.

In the week that followed, the determined citizens of Nevada City joined up with a vigilante group formed in Virginia City to rid the country of outlaws. Four more of Plummer's road agents were seized and hung from cottonwood trees, where they swung in the winter breezes, frozen stiff as icicles. Before he dropped, one of them told everything he knew about Henry Plummer and his outlaw band.

In the meantime, a vigilante committee had quietly formed in Bannack, the sheriff's home town. On January 10, someone noticed that the horses belonging to Plummer and his deputies were being brought into town. It appeared that the sheriff and his gang might be preparing to leave before the storm broke, and immediate action was decided upon.

The vigilantes rode to the rooming house where Plummer lived and, jerking him out of bed, informed him coldly that he was to be hanged immediately. Meantime, two others of the gang had been captured. The sheriff pleaded for his life, insisting that he was innocent, but the vigilantes had had enough and would not listen. Across the street stood the improvised gallows that Henry Plummer had built for the execution of a political enemy who was later proved innocent of the faked charge. Here the three bandits were hanged without further ado.

Thus died Montana's most infamous peace officer.

PAT GARRETT

PAT GARRETT

21.
PAT GARRETT
THE SHERIFF WHO SLEW BILLY THE KID

"QUIÉN ES?"

When Sheriff Pat Garrett of Lincoln County, New Mexico, heard these whispered words—who is it?—at midnight on the porch of Pete Maxwell's ranch house in Fort Sumner, he knew that his life depended on his quickness on the draw in the next few seconds. For the speaker was Billy the Kid, the Southwest's last and most notorious desperado. The answer the Kid got was a blast from his old friend's shotgun. It was the first time the Kid had ever been dropped on, and he never knew who did it.

His death on the warm summer evening of July 14, 1881, marked *finis* to the bloodiest years in the history of New Mexico and the Southwest.

While lawlessness certainly didn't depart into the grave with Billy the Kid, his reign of terror had made people in the Territory of New Mexico realize that he and others like him would have to go in order to make the country safe for the thousands of settlers who were pouring into the West.

With Billy's death a competent but hitherto undistinguished sheriff gained nationwide fame and more or less inherited his victim's mantle of notoriety. Pat Garrett was of the stern stuff that the best Western peace officers were made. He hung around with and counted among his friends many of the outlaws of the day but, given the job of tracking one of them down, he set out to do just that, with no hard feelings but with a firm determination to succeed. He was a hard fighter but no killer, earning in all only three notches for his gun—for Billy the Kid and two of his cronies, Tom O'Folliard and Charlie Bowdre.

Pat was twenty-eight when he drifted into the Pecos Valley and appeared, a dusty unprepossessing figure, on Pete Maxwell's front porch asking for a job. Pete was one of the richest men in the Southwest at the time, and his house in Fort Sumner, an abandoned Army town on the banks of the muddy Pecos River, was a gathering place for men from all over the region—cow punchers, outlaws, cattlemen. He looked Pat over and decided to give him a try.

His new cowboy turned out to be as good as he claimed and indeed he should have been. He had come from three years of buffalo hunting in the Panhandle. Before that he had spent some six years on a cattle ranch in Texas learning everything about the rough wild life of a cow puncher—a congenial life for the bold adventurous boy who had left behind him in Louisiana the shreds of the huge plantations his father had had before the Civil War.

Pat stayed on for six months at the Maxwell ranch and then, after a slight disagreement with Pete, he left and went into business for himself. For a time he ran a small restaurant and then he joined Beaver Smith running a general store and saloon. Pretty soon he was a part of the life of Fort Sumner and a solid citizen.

Along about this time Pat met Billy the Kid who was also a friend of Pete Maxwell's. Pat and the Kid got on well together—a strange combination, the tall, gaunt, easygoing Southerner and the tense, slight, gray-eyed Kid.

Billy the Kid was now, at eighteen, a full-fledged outlaw. He was notorious throughout the country, so much so that in August of 1878 the Governor of the Territory, General Lew Wallace, had made a special trip across the dusty trails of New Mexico to ask the young outlaw to lay down his arms. Billy refused. It was too late then for him to change his ways, and it had probably been too late since his early 'teens

for he had taken young to a life of violence and crime.

There are probably more conflicting stories about Billy the Kid than about any Western desperado. Today he is almost a folk hero. In the 1880's he was loved by many people and he had loyal friends. There is no doubt that he was a killer of the most deadly type, merciless and fearless and lightning quick on the draw. At the time of his death he claimed to have killed a man for every year of his age—twenty-one men, "not counting Indians and Mexicans."

The Kid was born William H. Bonney far from the wild frontier in New York City on November 23, 1859. Shortly afterwards his family went west, ending up in the old Spanish town of Santa Fe in New Mexico. There Billy lived and played until he was eight years old. Then the family moved to the rough and lawless town of Silver City where Billy went to school but learned far more from the gamblers and outlaws who infested the town. Finally when he was twelve he took the first step on his outlaw career by killing a man who had insulted his mother.

In the next few years he worked on cattle ranches in Arizona and New Mexico, he roamed down into Mexico itself, and in general he led a carefree, irresponsible life. He was a slender boy, about five feet eight inches tall, gray-eyed, and more fair than dark. Perhaps it was his youthful smiling appearance in a land of tough hardbitten men that inspired a friend of his to dub him "the Kid." Whatever its origin, the name stuck.

It was not until the Lincoln County war that the Kid came into his own as a killer and fighter; then it became apparent that he was more than a good cowboy quick with his trigger finger. The Lincoln County war was one of the bloodiest vendettas in all the annals of the frontier West. It was so serious that men were working as far away as Washington to bring it to an end. It was a fitting stage for the rising of the last dark star of outlawry in the West.

Like the Pleasant Valley war in Arizona, the roots to this war went a long way back before the first blood was drawn. On one side of the struggle was former Major L. G. Murphy, cattleman, politician, businessman, and the richest man in the mountains of Lincoln County. At that time the county was much larger than it is now, some two hundred miles square. The town of Lincoln was its center and focal point. Here Murphy had a thriving general store, a saloon, and a hotel, and in general ruled the town's business. Murphy was a schemer and out for every possible dollar by fair means or foul. One of his projects was a cattle ranch, whose cows were known as the "miracle herd" because no matter how many were sold, the total of beef on the hoof remained the same.

John Chisum accused Murphy of replenishing his herd from Chisum's thousands. Murphy only laughed at the accusations, secure in his position as the most powerful man in the county.

John Chisum was without a doubt the biggest cattleman in New Mexico. He had homesteaded thousands of acres of land and his herds of cattle numbered in the tens of thousands. He lived in South Spring Ranch on the Pecos River in a spacious adobe house, surrounded with marvelous fruit trees and birds he had brought into the valley. For some time he tried without success to bring to trial Murphy's hirelings who stole his cattle, but Murphy had the county's Sheriff Brady in the palm of his hand, and no rustler stayed caught for long. Any rustler knew that if he did not kick down the jail door, it wouldn't be long before some of his friends rode into town and rescued him.

Finally a couple of the rustlers were caught who did not escape from the flimsy adobe jail, and Murphy called on his lawyer, Alexander A. McSween, to defend the men. But McSween was an unusual man in the godless West of the time. A minister turned lawyer, he was a deeply religious man who did not believe in the tough law of the frontier—an eye for an eye and a tooth for a tooth and more if you can get the draw quick enough. He was also an honest man and refused to take on the defense of these men so obviously guilty. That was the end of him for Murphy.

To add insult to injury for Murphy, John Chisum promptly hired McSween to prosecute the thieves. In the process of their conviction it was proved that they were indeed Murphy's hirelings and that they were in an organized business of buying cattle from other thieves who raided Chisum's herds.

Shortly afterwards McSween joined up with a jovial Englishman, J. H. Tunstall, to open a general store and bank in Lincoln. Murphy was infuriated at this open rivalry, and bad feeling grew more intense.

One morning in February 1878 the townspeople saw a posse of twenty men, led by Sheriff Brady, head out of town for Tunstall's ranch. Murphy had decided to take Tunstall and McSween down a peg or two by catching them on a vague legal charge.

The posse met Tunstall riding cheerfully along the trail into town. Before he could speak they shot him down in cold blood, wheeled their horses, and returned to town. On the hills beyond, too far away to come to their friend's help, were Billy the Kid and Dick Brewer. The next day the Kid stood grimly at Tunstall's grave, vowing to get every one of Tunstall's killers or die in the attempt.

Tunstall's death touched off the Lincoln County war. As the news of his murder spread, men donned their guns in towns and on ranches all over the county and rode into Lincoln to join up with either Murphy or McSween, as their fancy or allegiance took them. Billy had already put his guns at the service of McSween and coldly proceeded to wipe out as many of the men on the deadly posse as he could, including Sheriff Brady whom he shot down in cold blood.

The climax to the war came in July of the same year, with a fierce three days' battle which ended with the death of many men on both sides, including McSween, with the burning of the McSween house, and with Billy the Kid's miraculous escape from that burning house surrounded on all sides by trigger-happy Murphy men.

In the war right had been on no one side, although Murphy had had the law on his. The President in Washington was so concerned that he appointed General Lew Wallace governor and sent him out to see what he could do to quiet things down. An amnesty was offered to everyone on both sides of the fight who would

lay down his arms. No one had had much stomach for fighting since the long battle, and all were glad to stop the shooting war. Only Billy the Kid refused. Taking to the mountains and ranges around southwestern New Mexico, he became a topnotch cattle rustler and a menace to all honest cattlemen. He rode into Fort Sumner from time to time to whoop it up with his cronies when he was in the money.

Many influential men in the Territory now began to realize that lawlessness could not continue rampant in the area much longer. More and more settlers were coming west every day. Other territories were becoming states while New Mexico and Arizona were ignored because of their nationwide reputation for violence and danger. John Chisum and other big cattlemen got together and decided that the first step in cleaning up the Territory was the removal of Billy the Kid. Elections for county sheriff were approaching. They looked around for a reliable candidate who would be fearless and determined enough to go out after and capture the Kid. They chose Pat Garrett, who had the added advantage of familiarity with the ways and

haunts of his old crony. Pat accepted the offer and won the election.

In Sheriff Garrett's hunt for Billy help came from all quarters, for all sorts of agencies were interested in ridding the country of its principal outlaw. There were detectives for cattlemen's groups and a Secret Service man. The law was closing in on Billy the Kid.

It was Christmas Eve in 1880. Riding merrily into old Fort Sumner on their way to a holiday dance were six outlaws headed by Billy the Kid. On the way into town Billy left his friends, some sixth sense possibly warning him of danger. The next he heard of them was a blast of shooting from the old building where the dance was to be held.

In that building waited Pat Garrett and fifteen tough men. They were playing poker, smoking, and listening for the sound of hoofbeats on the road. Finally it came. Garrett and four of his men rushed outside, rifles cocked and ready. When the outlaws were only a few yards away, the men moved out into the road.

"Up with your hands!" yelled Garrett.

The first horseman moved to draw his six gun. Before he could get it out he was mortally shot by Garrett. The other four horsemen turned and rode away under a rain of fire from the rest of the posse. On the ground lay Tom O'Folliard dying. On a cold Christmas morning the first of Billy the Kid's good friends was buried outside of town in the midst of a raging blizzard.

By Christmas night the snow had stopped, and at midnight Garrett and his posse were ready to ride again. From the information he could gather he guessed that Billy and his friends would have holed up in an old sheepherder's hut at Stinking Spring. Just before dawn the posse arrived. In the dim light they could see three horses tethered outside the hut. There was no sign of life.

Silently the possemen took up positions around the house. Pat crept along an arroyo until he and three of his men were within about ten yards of the door and fully protected. Slowly

day began to break. The sun rose on the bleak snow-covered valley. The door opened and Charlie Bowdre stepped out to feed his horse.

Garrett raised his rifle to his shoulder.

"Come out with your hands up!" he called.

Bowdre started to grab his gun; almost before he had moved he was shot through and he stumbled back into the house. Before he could fall, the Kid grabbed him.

"Out there with you, Charlie. Take some of those hombres with you when you go."

Charlie was too far gone to lift his gun hand. He staggered out across the snow and blindly fell into the arroyo, his last words: "I wish . . . I wish . . . ."

Pat turned again to the cabin.

"You'd better give yourselves up, boys. We're going to stay here until you do. You haven't a chance."

"Not by a long shot, Pat," called Billy. "You just think you've got us."

All day the posse waited in the snow. They took turns going out to bring food

in from a near-by ranch. Finally their hunger and the cold were too much for the four outlaws. In the evening a white handkerchief was shoved out the window. Out onto the hardpacked snow came the Kid and his three companions, their hands up, caught at last.

The next day Charlie Bowdre was buried in the little cemetery beside Tom O'Folliard. Two of the Kid's oldest friends were now underground.

Sheriff Garrett escorted his charges across the wintry trails to Las Vegas where they took the train to Santa Fe, and later to Mesilla in March. On the way Pat and Billy joshed one another as they had while hanging around saloons together only a few short years before. Now that they no longer had to fight it out, there was no point in not being friendly—until Billy saw a chance to escape, that is.

In Mesilla Billy was tried and convicted of the murder of Sheriff Brady three years before in the Lincoln County war. He was sentenced to be hanged in Lincoln on May 13, 1881. Back over the mountains to Lincoln rode Billy the Kid, accompanied by two of Pat's deputies, genial, pleasant J. W. Bell and the cruel, overbearing Bob Ollinger who hated Billy and lost no opportunity to taunt him about the rope that awaited him only two months hence.

Through March and April the Kid lived in the Lincoln County courthouse, shackled hand and foot and watched day and night by deputy sheriffs Bell and Ollinger. Pat Garrett looked in on the prisoner from day to day, watchful that his elusive captive would not escape. Ollinger never ceased doing all he could to torment Billy, and Billy smiled with his cold gray eyes and gave his hated tormentor no satisfaction. Bell, on the other hand, was a kindly man who could see no harm in enjoying a few hands of monte or poker with Billy and passing pleasantly the lengthening warm days of spring.

On the morning of April 28 Pat looked in to say he was riding over to White Oaks to see about the gallows for the hanging in May. At noon Ollinger strolled out to a saloon, leaving his shotgun behind. No one ever knew quite what happened in the next hour, until suddenly

a shot snapped the quiet of the town. Ollinger heard it in LaRue's saloon. He put down his glass and stepped out into the dusty sunny street. There wasn't a sound. Almost running he approached the courthouse. "It couldn't be that Billy . . ."

He never had time to finish his thought.

"Hey there, Bob," came a soft voice from the second floor of the courthouse. Bob Ollinger looked up. There was Billy holding his, Bob's, shotgun. The next instant Ollinger lay on the ground dead.

Not a soul stirred in Lincoln that afternoon. Shutters were closed and doors were bolted. Billy the Kid rolled a cigarette, picked up some guns from the armory in the courthouse, caught himself a horse, and rode out of town as leisurely as the most upright citizen. No one moved to stop him. When he had been gone some time, people came out of doors and went into the courthouse, to find Bell dead on the stairs and cards scattered on the floor of the room where Billy had been kept. A Mexican rode out to White Oaks carrying the word to Pat Garrett.

Pat was a philosophical soul. Well, he had lost his man. But he had caught him once, he could catch him again. Now he knew it was a question between him and the Kid of who could shoot first, for Billy would never again be taken alive.

Through May and June Pat sent posses out over a vast area of the country. No Billy. Then Pat settled back to wait. He knew word would come sometime, somehow. When it did come, he hardly believed it for the rumor was that Billy was hanging around Fort Sumner—all but under their noses. It couldn't hurt to follow a rumor to Fort Sumner, and on the evening of July 13 Garrett set off for the town with two of his deputies, John W. Poe and Tip McKinney.

The next day Poe rode into town to see what news he could pick up. No one was willing to talk; no one cared to mention Billy. It looked like a cold trail. That evening Poe rejoined Pat and McKinney, and they decided to make a last try at Pete Maxwell's to see if he knew anything.

It was midnight when the three men got to Pete's. Poe and McKinney sat on the steps of the porch and lit cigarettes. Pat slipped

quietly into Pete's bedroom off the porch and bent down to wake Pete. Across the lawn came a shadowy figure, slipping along quietly and casually in his stocking feet. He was almost upon Poe and McKinney before he saw them. Swiftly alert to danger he stiffened, his hand on his gun, and backed away.

"*Quién es?*" he whispered.

Poe and McKinney, certain that their quarry was miles away, thought it was only a Mexican sheepherder.

"Take it easy, fellow," said Poe. "We don't aim to hurt you."

The slim shadow backed up to the door of Pete's room. He moved inside and, turning, called again,

"*Quién es?*"

At the first sound of the voice outside, Pat had frozen. His hand went to his gun. He had recognized Billy's voice as Poe and McKinney had not. Before Billy had time to make out the dark form beside Pete's bed, Pat's gun roared into the midnight stillness, and Billy the Kid lay dead.

The next day the whole of Fort Sumner turned out for the funeral of their most distinguished desperado. Billy the Kid was laid to rest beside Charlie Bowdre and Tom O'Folliard, three narrow dusty graves which are today unmarked and almost unknown except by the few oldtimers who are left alive to remember.

Overnight Pat Garrett became famous. Fortunately he was a sturdy, humorous frontiersman and it didn't turn his head. Unlike most gun-toting peace officers, however, Pat wrote a book. After the death of Billy the Kid there were many controversial stories in magazines, newspapers, and books of the Kid's life. In 1882 there appeared *The Authentic Life of Billy the Kid* by Pat F. Garrett.

At the end of his term in Lincoln County Pat gave up his sheriff's badge and went back to cattle ranching, but the spirit of the peace officer could not be laid to rest so easily. For a time he managed a cattle detective agency in the Panhandle. He was a captain in the Texas Rangers, and he was sheriff of Doña Ana County. In 1901 President Theodore Roosevelt met Pat and, taking a fancy to him, got him appointed to the job of Collector of Customs at the border station at El Paso. Finally Pat settled in Las Cruces, New Mexico, and there in 1908 he was killed by a stockman while riding the range, under mysterious circumstances that have never been satisfactorily cleared up.

So died with his boots on the last great sheriff of the frontier who had in his hour of glory brought down the greatest desperado of the West.

BIBLIOGRAPHY

Adams, Ward R.: *History of Arizona,* Record Publishing Co., Phoenix, Arizona, 1930.

Barnes, William Croft: *Apaches and Longhorns,* Anderson & Ritchie, Los Angeles, 1941. Reminiscences.

Birney, Hoffman: *Vigilantes,* Penn Publishing Co., Philadelphia, 1929. A chronicle of the rise and fall of the Plummer gang of outlaws in and about Virginia City, Montana, in the early '60's.

Botkin, B. A., editor: *A Treasury of American Folklore,* Crown Publishers, 1944.

Breakenridge, William M.: *Helldorado,* Houghton, 1928.

Burns, Walter Noble: *The Saga of Billy the Kid,* Doubleday, 1925, 1926.

———. *Tombstone,* Doubleday, 1927.

Burt, Struthers: *Powder River, Let 'Er Buck,* Farrar, 1938.

Bushick, Frank H.: *Glamorous Days,* Naylor Co., San Antonio, 1934.

Canton, Frank M.: *Frontier Trails,* Houghton, 1930. Autobiography.

Coblentz, Stanton A.: *Villains and Vigilantes,* Wilson-Erickson, Elmira, N. Y., 1936.

Coe, George W.: *Frontier Fighter,* Houghton, 1934. Autobiography by a man who rode and fought with Billy the Kid.

Collins, Hubert E.: *Warpath and Cattle Trail,* with a foreword by Hamlin Garland, Morrow, 1928.

Connelley, William Elsey: *Wild Bill and His Era,* Press of the Pioneers, Elmira, N. Y., 1930.

Cook, James H.: *Fifty Years on the Old Frontier, as cowboy, hunter, guide, scout, and ranchman,* Yale University Press, 1923.

Dick, Everett: *Vanguards of the Frontier,* Appleton-Century, 1941. A social history of the northern plains and Rocky Mountains.

Dimsdale, Thomas J.: *The Vigilantes of Montana,* 1882; University of Oklahoma Press, 1953.

Dobie, J. Frank: *Guide to Life and Literature of the Southwest,* University Press in Dallas, 1943.

———. *A Vaquero of the Brush Country,* Southwest Press, 1929; Little, Brown, 1943.

Eisele, Wilbert E.: *The Real Wild Bill Hickok, famous scout and knight chivalric of the plains,* W. H. Andre, 1931. A true story of pioneer life in the Far West.

Emrich, Duncan: *It's An Old Wild West Custom,* Vanguard, 1949.

Farish, Thomas Edwin: *History of Arizona,* commissioned by the State Legislature, 1915.

Forrest, Earle R.: *Arizona's Dark and Bloody Ground,* Caxton Printers, 1936.

Fuller, Henry C.: *A Texas Sheriff,* Baker, 1931.

Gard, Wayne: *Frontier Justice,* University of Oklahoma Press, 1949.

Garrett, Pat F.: *The Authentic Life of Billy the Kid,* 1882; 1954 edition, University of Oklahoma Press.

Gipson, Fred: *Fabulous Empire,* Houghton, 1946.

Grinnell, George Bird: *Beyond the Old Frontier,* Scribner, 1913, 1950.

Guernsey, Charles A.: *Wyoming Cowboy Days,* Putnam, 1936.

Hafen, Le Roy, and Rister, C. C.: *Western America,* Prentice-Hall, 1941.

Haley, J. Evetts: *Jeff Milton,* University of Oklahoma Press, 1948.

Halsell, H. H.: *Cowboys and Cattleland,* published by the author, Lubbock, Texas, 1937.

Hanson, Joseph Mills: *The Conquest of the Missouri,* McClurg, 1909.

Hardin, John Wesley: *The Life of John Wesley Hardin,* Gammel's Book Store, Austin, Texas, 1896. Autobiography.

Hough, Emerson: *The Story of the Cowboy,* Appleton, 1912; Grosset & Dunlap, 1925.

——. *The Story of the Outlaw,* Burt, 1910; Grosset & Dunlap, 1925.

Hunter, J. Marvin: *The Trail Drivers of Texas,* Cokesbury Press, 1927. True stories by real cowpunchers.

Jennings, N. A.: *A Texas Ranger,* Scribner, 1899.

Keleher, William A.: *The Fabulous Frontier,* Rydal Press, Santa Fe, 1945.

Lake, Stuart N.: *Wyatt Earp: Frontier Marshal,* Houghton Mifflin Co., 1931.

Langford, Nathaniel Pitt: *Vigilante Days and Ways,* McClurg, 1912. The makers and making of Montana and Idaho.

Lockwood, Frank C.: *Pioneer Days in Arizona,* Macmillan, 1932.

McCoy, Joseph G.: *Historic Sketches of the Cattle Trails of the West and Southwest,* Rare Book Shop, Washington, 1932.

McDonald, A. B.: *Hands Up!,* Bobbs, 1927. Stories of the six-gun fighters of the old Wild West as told by Fred E. Sutton.

McNeal, T. A.: *When Kansas Was Young,* Macmillan, 1922.

Mercer, Asa Shinn: *The Banditti of the Plains,* 1930; University of Oklahoma Press, 1954.

Monaghan, Jay: *Last of the Bad Men,* Bobbs-Merrill, 1946.

Myers, John Myers: *The Tombstone Story,* Grosset & Dunlap, Inc., 1951. Published as *The Last Chance,* Dutton, 1950.

Osgood, Ernest Staples: *The Day of the Cattleman,* University of Minnesota Press, 1929.

Otero, Miguel Antonio: *The Real Billy the Kid,* R. W. Wilson, Elmira, N. Y., 1936.

——. *My Life on the Frontier,* Wilson-Erickson, Elmira, N. Y., 1935. Autobiography.

Paxson, Frederic L.: *History of the American Frontier, 1763–1893,* Houghton, 1924.

Pelzer, Louis: *The Cattlemen's Frontier,* A. H. Clark, Glendale, Calif., 1936.

Poe, John W.: *The Death of Billy the Kid,* Houghton, 1933.

Poe, Sophie A.: *Buckboard Days,* Caxton Printers, Caldwell, Idaho, 1936.

Raine, William MacLeod: *Famous Sheriffs and Western Outlaws,* Garden City, 1944.

——. *Guns of the Frontier,* World, 1946.

——. *Texas Ranger,* Grosset & Dunlap, 1917.

——. and Barnes, Will C.: *Cattle,* Doubleday, Doran, 1930; Grosset & Dunlap, 1936.

Ripley, Thomas: *They Died with Their Boots On,* Doubleday, 1935.

Robson, William A.: *Civilization and the Growth of Law,* Macmillan, 1935.

Roosevelt, Theodore: *Stories of the Great West,* Century, 1909; Appleton-Century, 1940.

——. *The Winning of the West,* Putnam, 1920.

Sabin, Edwin L.: *Wild Men of the Wild West,* Crowell, 1929.

Siringo, Charles A.: *The History of Billy the Kid* (revision).

——. *Riata and Spurs,* Houghton, 1931. Autobiography.

Sonnichsen, Charles L.: *Billy King's Tombstone,* Caxton Printers, 1942.

——. *Roy Bean—Law West of the Pecos,* Macmillan, 1943.

Streeter, Floyd Benjamin; *Prairie Towns and Cow Trails,* Chapman & Grimes, Boston, 1936.

Sutley, Zachary Taylor: *The Last Frontier,* Macmillan, 1930.

Targ, William, editor: *The American West,* World, 1946.

Taylor, Bayard: *Eldorado, or Adventures in the Path of Empire,* Putnam, 1912(?). Knopf, 1949.

Tilghman, Zoe A.: *Outlaw Days in Oklahoma,* Harlow Pub. Co., Oklahoma City, 1925.

Turner, Frederick Jackson: *The Frontier in American History,* Holt, 1921.

——. *List of references on the History of the West,* 3rd. ed., Harvard University Press, 1916.

Vestal, Stanley: *Queen of Cowtowns, Dodge City: the wickedest little city in America, 1872–86,* Harper, 1952.

Walters, Lorenzo D.: *Tombstone's Yesterday,* Acme Printing Co., Tucson, Arizona, 1928.

Walton, W. M.: *Life and Adventures of Ben Thompson, the Famous Texan, including a detailed and authentic statement of his birth, history and adventures by one who has known him as a child,* Frontier Press of Texas, Houston, 1954.

Webb, Walter Prescott: *The Texas Rangers,* Houghton Mifflin, 1935.

——. *The Great Plains,* Ginn, 1931.

Wellman, Paul I.: *The Trampling Herd,* Doubleday, 1951.

Wilstach, Frank J.: *Wild Bill Hickok,* Doubleday, Page, 1926.

Wright, Robert M.: *Dodge City, the Cowboy Capital,* Shakespeare Press, N. Y., 1913.

Yoakum, Henderson: *History of Texas,* Steck Publishers, Austin, Texas, 1935. Original narratives of Texas history and adventure.

INDEX